The
Gourmet's Guide To
CHOCOLATE

The Gourmet's Guide To CHOCOLATE

Lesly Berger

QUILL
New York 1984

Library of Congress Catalog Card Number: 84-42597

ISBN: 0-688-02501-3

The Gourmet's Guide to Chocolate
was produced and prepared by
Quarto Marketing Ltd.
212 Fifth Avenue, New York, N.Y. 10010

Editor: Naomi Black
Art Director: Richard Boddy
Designer: Mary Moriarty
Editorial Assistant: Mary Forsell
Cover Design: Liz Trovato
Cover Photograph: Maria Robledo
Illustrations: Kurt J. Wallace

Typeset by BPE Graphics, Inc.
Printed and bound in the United States by
Interstate Book Manufacturers, Inc.

First Quill Edition
1 2 3 4 5 6 7 8 9 10

DEDICATION

To Michael and William Paul, with love and chocolate kisses

ACKNOWLEDGMENTS

I would like to thank those in the chocolate and confectionery industry, too numerous to mention here, who took the time to assist me in my research for this book and who generously provided me with samples of their wares.

Special thanks go to a discriminating and dedicated group of chocolate tasters: Adrienne Berger, Fredlynn Jeck, Bob Knox, Kirsten Mishkin, and Michael Meyerson.

Thanks are also due to Alan Schnapp, who helped in the later stages of this book.

ABOUT THE AUTHOR

LESLY BERGER IS A NEW YORK CITY-BASED FREELANCE WRITER, WHOSE ARTICLES have appeared in such popular journals as *The New York Times, Self, Working Woman, Mademoiselle, Seventeen,* and *Family Weekly.* As a former editor for *Glamour* magazine, she wrote articles on subjects as diverse as health, psychology, sports, recreation, and humor. She was educated at Hampshire and Vassar colleges.

Contents

How to Use this Book

THIS BOOK IS A GUIDE TO THE BEST CHOCOLATES FROM A DOZEN NATIONS. IT describes each country's basic chocolate-making style as well as variations on the theme. Not every chocolate maker is listed here; those who are within these pages represent the crème de la crème of chocolate—the truly delicious, innovative, and exciting examples of the chocolate maker's artistry. However, the fact that your favorite chocolatier may not have been included does not necessarily mean that he or she is in disfavor. In the rapidly growing and changing world of chocolate, it is simply impossible to acknowledge every worthy participant. To paraphrase Mae West, "So many chocolates, so little time."

The chocolates included are not ranked. No ratings with cute little chocolate kisses or stars were deemed necessary or appropriate, for two reasons. First, as they are fond of saying at Harvard, all who have survived the primary selection process are more than eminently qualified. Second, chocolate is, and should remain, a highly individual (if not idiosyncratic) pleasure. This book does not intend to deprive you of such a marvelous opportunity to make your own judgments—it gives you the necessary information as to ingredients, styles, and distinguishing characteristics—but it is finally up to you, the consumer, to provide the ultimate test of taste.

For those of you who live far from any chocolate outlet, the sinful sweets are still within reach. Find the chocolates that most intrigue you, then turn to the "Sources" section in the back of the book. You will truly discover a world of delight, as most of these places accept mail or telephone orders.

Introduction

PERFECTION IS NOT EASY TO COME BY. A PARK AVENUE TOWNHOUSE WILL SET YOU back $2.5 million; a properly equipped Rolls Royce Silver Cloud (cocktail tables included) can easily clear $110,000; even a champion-sired Lhasa apso puppy (without a jeweled collar) goes to the tune of $425. However, for anywhere between eighty cents and a dollar, you can become the proud owner of a modern masterpiece, a luscious luxury, a sensually sybaritic imported Swiss chocolate champagne truffle.

We are in the midst of a chocolate renaissance, a veritable confection-ery age of enlightenment. Gone are the days of banal assortments whose main ingredient seemed to be grainy sugar with chocolate flavoring and brown bars that seemed to lack any chocolate at all. Now a plethora of chocolate products has burst onto the scene, and gourmet chefs are creating chocolate culinary classics. From the simplest molded milk chocolate teddy bear to the most sophisticated blends of bittersweet chocolate, Grand Marnier, and buttery hazelnut praline, chocolate has grown up.

This guide is a celebration of chocolate and its exhilarating newfound maturity. It will take you back to the dark ages of the B.C. (before chocolate) period, and educate you as to the history of the humble cacao bean and its glorious evolution into the spectacular substance we know and love today. It will enable you to visit the world's great chocolate-making capitals and compare the arts and specialties of each. It will provide you with useful information on cooking with chocolate, and above all, will turn you into an educated chocolate consumer. Lastly, it will take you on a shop-by-shop tour of some of the world's most exclusive chocolatiers.

This book does not pretend to be the last word on chocolate; rather, it is a guidebook that will help you turn your love affair with chocolate into a deep and passionate lasting relationship.

The Story of Chocolate

THE STORY OF CHOCOLATE BEGINS IN 600 A.D. IN THE JUNGLES OF THE YUCATAN, where the Mayas established the earliest known plantation for growing cacao (the tree which produces the famed cocoa bean). Even at this early date, cocoa beans were valuable commodities, to which mystical and religious significance was ascribed. The beans were used throughout Central America both as forms of payment and as units of calculation. For example, four hundred cocoa beans constituted one *zontli*, while eight thousand made up one *xiquipilli*. But their most important function was, not surprisingly, culinary. After being roasted, ground, combined with liquid, and beaten until frothy, cocoa beans served as the main component of a foamy drink called *chocolatl*. This bitter, rather

In the Aztec emperor Montezuma's court, the drinking of
chocolatl, sometimes made with a wine base, was
considered a religious experience.

11

unappetizing concoction bore remarkably little resemblance (except in its foamy appearance) to the sweet and soothing cocoa we enjoy today. Yet, the uniquely pleasing taste properties of even this early, unrefined chocolate had already begun to work their magic on Central American Indian consumers.

By the year 1200, the Aztecs had conquered the Mayas and Toltecs. In recognition of their supremacy over the rest of Central America, the Aztecs imposed deliveries of cocoa beans as tribute from conquered tribes. Later, in the court of renowned Aztec Emperor Montezuma, cocoa became the favored beverage for the Emperor himself and for his privileged intimates. The drink was flavored with vanilla and drunk out of ornate golden goblets—at the reputed rate of fifty large jars a day for the court alone!

But chocolate was too precious a commodity to remain the exclusive property of the New World. It somehow seems fitting that not only did Christopher Columbus discover America, he also has the distinction of being the first European to discover cocoa beans. In 1502, on his fourth voyage to the New World, Columbus landed in Nicaragua and saw cocoa beans in use as currency. He also encountered the natives drinking chocolate. Although Columbus had the foresight to bring several specimens of the beans back to King Ferdinand's court in Spain, he lacked the true gourmet's instinct. Perhaps as a consequence, cacao was not considered by the Spaniards to be of any importance. But that view was soon to change.

The intrepid Spanish explorer Hernando Cortez, during his successful conquest of Mexico in 1519, is thought to have been the first European actually to have tasted chocolate. Ironically, the drink itself did not please him, but because of the high esteem in which the natives held it, he wisely assumed it would soon be a valuable item throughout the world. Thus Cortez quickly set about establishing his own cocoa plantation, as an early example of a "money crop." All proceeds from this venture were earmarked for his native Spain.

In 1528 Cortez traveled to Spain, bearing utensils for the preparation of drinking chocolate along with the first cocoa to be used for European consumption. The Spaniards took to the drink in no time, using a recipe similar to that favored by the Aztecs, but added chilies and other hot spices to the still-bitter brew.

Historians disagree as to the exact chronology, but at some point sugar was added to the other ingredients. At last, chocolate drinkers were on the right track. With this essential addition, cocoa became infinitely more palatable and consequently gained in popularity. Spain began to plant more cacao in its overseas territories. Meanwhile, the Spanish aristocracy remained the sole European cocoa consumers; they kept this exclusive potion—which they later heated and drank with cinnamon as well as vanilla—a secret for almost a century.

In 1615 cocoa finally found its way to France, in what any gourmet today would have to see as the best and most far-reaching result of the marriage of Spanish princess Anna of Austria, daughter of King Philip III, to King Louis XIII of France. Under Anna's instructions, chocolate was served at the French court. As with most matters of French court etiquette, chocolate eventually became the fashion throughout France.

The first recorded drinking of chocolate in England took place in the ever-knowledgeable community of Oxford in 1650. Toward the end of the seventeenth century, chocolate had arrived in Belgium, Germany, and Switzerland. Soon after, cocoa was brought to Austria and Italy, finally reaching America in 1755. Coffee houses that served cocoa opened and continued to gain in popularity throughout eighteenth century England. In their function as meeting places, these houses served as precursors to the bars and cafes of modern times. At the peak of the craze, there were coffee houses for every sort of clientele, be they gamblers, politicians, literati, or fashionable folk.

At this time chocolate was still being prepared by hand—an arduous and inefficient process. In 1795 Bristol's Dr. Joseph Fry (a name still important to British chocolate lovers today) was the first Englishman to manufacture chocolate on a large scale, using a steam engine to grind the beans. Then, in 1828, Dutch chocolate maker C. J. Van Houten invented the cocoa press, which squeezed out part of the cocoa butter from the beans, thus creating a smoother, more appetizing beverage. Van Houten's other valuable contribution to the art of chocolate was called (for obvious reasons) "Dutching." This is an alkalinizing process that neutralizes the natural acid found in cocoa powder, resulting in a more easily digestible drink.

Chocolate was beginning to develop a refined taste that might be recognizable today. Perhaps the two most important new developments in chocolatedom took place, appropriately enough, in Switzerland, which to this day many consider the chocolate center of the world. In 1875 Daniel Peter, after eight years of experimentation, succeeded in adding condensed milk to chocolate, perfecting a solid milk chocolate that could be used for eating. In 1879 Rodolphe Lindt, an eccentric Berne aristocrat, invented a truly revolutionary new way of refining chocolate. Lindt's process, known as "conching," consisted of placing the chocolate into a heated trough while a roller moved back and forth through it for seventy-two hours. Conching, plus the addition of extra cocoa butter to the now especially smooth chocolate, created the original "fondant," or melting chocolate, the smoothness of which effectively did away with the old-fashioned, coarse-grained, gritty stuff. This delicious new chocolate could be poured into molds (previously it had to be pressed into the molds), paving the way for making chocolate confectionery as we know it today. To be sure, other advances in machinery and technology were—and are—still to come, but at that point chocolate actually became the creamy, versatile substance that is still sweetening our lives today.

The Science of Chocolate

IN 1775, IN RECOGNITION OF ITS UNIQUE PROPERTIES, SWEDISH NATURALIST CAROLUS Linnaeus renamed the cacao tree *Theobroma*, which is a Greek term meaning, "Food of the Gods." Luckily, one may be a mere mortal and still enjoy chocolate; whether eaten or drunk, the celebrated stuff is one of life's great pleasures. However, as with all truly good things, the delights of chocolate have been somewhat dimmed by certain doomsayers who exaggerate its ill effects. But, as the lover says on St. Valentine's Day, "Take heart." These days the news about chocolate is actually surprisingly good. So that you can continue swallowing those bonbons and quaffing that cocoa in good conscience, here are some scientific facts about chocolate's nutritional value, effects on the teeth and skin, and other chemical characteristics.

While chocolate is not, alas, a necessary part of a healthy diet (this refers to nutritional—not psychological—health), neither is it as harmful as we may have been led to believe. Chocolate does contain certain essential nutrients, such as protein, carbohydrates, and fats; minerals such as calcium and iron; and vitamins such as thiamine and riboflavin. When milk, nuts, or fruits are added to chocolate, it becomes even more nutritionally sound.

The concerns of the weight conscious in reality have little to do with the chocolate itself. The true villain is the sugar content of chocolate, which makes it high in calories. Yet there is good news. The more expensive the chocolate, the lower its sugar content is likely to be, and thus the less caloric. For the creative, this can be an excellent excuse for splurging.

But what about teeth? Though your parents may have threatened to take away your chocolate allowance after a bad report from the dentist, research now shows that chocolate bars may not have been the cavity-causing culprits they were once labeled. Incredibly, scientists have found that instead of contributing to cavities, chocolate might actually help *prevent* tooth decay. Apparently, chocolate's fat content, plus a certain anti-decay-forming substance within the cocoa bean itself, acts to inhibit the decay-causing effects of the sugar in chocolate, and consequently protect the teeth against cavities and dental plaque. (Carob, that poor substitute for real chocolate, on the other hand, was found to be five times more likely than milk chocolate to cause tooth decay—so there is some justice in this world.) So keep brushing, flossing, and visiting your dentist—and don't feel guilty about having another chocolate!

Recently, much has been made of the caffeine content of chocolate, which has been blamed for jumpiness and irritability. But chocolate actually contains far less caffeine than coffee. One ounce of bittersweet chocolate has 5–10 milligrams of caffeine, an ounce of milk chocolate has 5 milligrams, and one 6-ounce cup of cocoa has ten milligrams—as opposed to the 100–150 milligrams of caffeine found in one cup of brewed coffee. Therefore, those trying to cut down on caffeine would do better to eliminate the coffee from their diets and spare the chocolate. Chocolate does contain another chemical, theobromine, which acts as a stimulant and diuretic, but has still been found to be less jitter-inspiring than coffee can be.

Now for the teenage bugaboo, acne. No more deprivation before the

Chocolate and Love

For many, the food of love par excellence has been and always will be chocolate. Legend has it that Emperor Montezuma himself drank chocolatl *before paying a visit to his harem. The wily fellow also served his favorite beverage to maidens who were brought to his court as offerings. Additionally, the Aztecs were said to consume great quantities of* chocolatl *in conjunction with religious ceremonies honoring Xochiquetzal, whom they worshipped as their goddess of love.*

XOCHIQUETZAL

By the seventeenth century, chocolate's powers as an aphrodisiac were touted by no less than Madame du Barry, who fed it to her boyfriends, and Casanova, who seduced countless women with its help. Other less well-known (though presumably no less successful) practi-

high school prom—scientists have found no correlation between chocolate and pimples. It's that simple. Such conservative health authorities as the American Medical Association have said that even consuming large amounts of chocolate has no demonstrable effect on acne sufferers. Thus, those who stay home alone on Saturday nights due to poorly timed breakouts may at least console themselves by munching on chocolate while waiting for their skin to clear.

tioners of the game of love also attributed remarkable sensual properties to chocolate.

CASANOVA

Even today, chocolate is the favored gift for lovers, not just in adorable frilly hearts on St. Valentine's Day, but all year round. And as it turns out, there just might be a scientific reason why chocolate is associated so powerfully with love and desire. Studies have shown that chocolate contains phenylethylamine, a chemical stimulant that is also released by the brain when people fall in love or are infatuated. Thus, some people believe that consuming chocolate replicates, to some degree, the physical effects of falling in love (although studies have shown this to be somewhat misleading).

Correspondingly, those who end a love affair and thus "fall out of love," experience lowered levels of phenylethylamine in the brain. These former lovers feel almost as if they are in the throes of withdrawal symptoms, due to lack of the chemical stimulant. For this reason, a scorned sweetheart may choose to drown his or her sorrows by going on a chocolate binge—which not only delights the tongue, but soothes the brain by delivering to it extra doses of that missing phenylethylamine.

Remember, then, that whether you are delightfully head-over-heels in love or have crash-landed into a world without love, to paraphrase the Bard: "If chocolate be the food of love, eat on."

How Chocolate is Grown and Manufactured

GROWTH

ONE OF THE REASONS THAT CHOCOLATE IS SUCH A PRECIOUS COMMODITY IS THAT the cacao tree from which it is made is, like most true chocolate lovers, extremely sensitive. The cacao tree needs intense heat and moisture, and it thrives only in a tropical climate. Therefore, its cultivation is limited to those areas within twenty degrees north or south of the equator, including central and northern South America, central and western Africa, and parts of southeast Asia.

The tree itself, especially when young, must be protected not only from wind, but also from direct sunlight. Because cacao trees require a substantial amount of shade, shade trees such as banana trees, coconut palms, lemon trees, and baobab are often planted nearby. In grateful recognition of the crucial caretaking function these shade trees perform, they are called "cocoa mothers."

Due to their delicate nature, cacao seedlings are usually given their start not outdoors in the cruel world, but indoors in the gentler environment of a nursery or greenhouse, where they are planted in rush baskets. After several months of nurturing, the young plants, along with their baskets, are ready to join their families and friends, and are transplanted outside in the plantation.

In their second year, many trees begin to produce pink and white waxy-looking blossoms. As befitting such a singular tree, these blossoms appear directly on the tree trunks, rather than on the branches.

By their third or fourth year, some precocious trees are already bearing ripe fruit, in the form of pods, which can be picked. The trees grow rapidly. A mature cultivated tree will reach a height of about twenty feet, while wild cacao trees may reach heights as great as over sixty feet.

By their fifth year, cacao trees of almost every variety are producing pickable pods. These pods appear on the tree's trunk and main branches. They can be either green or dark red, and have an oval or elongated shape, somewhat resembling cucumbers. The pods range in size from 6 to 10 inches in length and from 3 to 4 inches in diameter. When the pods ripen, their hard outer shells turn golden or bright red.

It is inside the pods, nestled amid a whitish pulp, that the almond-shaped cocoa beans are found. Each pod contains anywhere from 20 to 50 beans, which may be flat or somewhat rounded. These beans usually range in size from ½ to 1¼ inches long, ½ to ¾ inches wide, and ⅓ to ½ inch thick.

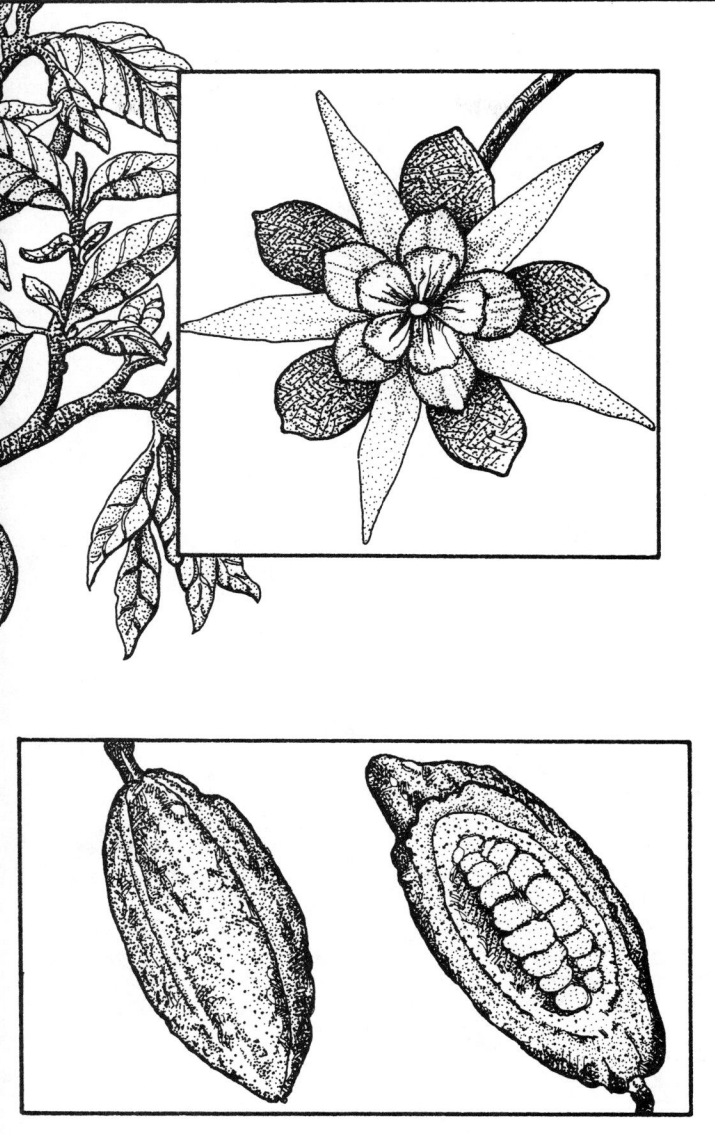

The cocoa tree (left) produces lustrous, green leaves, and
dainty yellow flowers (top right) but is most highly prized
for its fruit, the bulbous seed-laden pods that hang directly
from the tree's trunk (bottom left). When the pod is split
in two, the ripe bean can be harvested (bottom right).

MAJOR
COCOA-PRODUCING
COUNTRIES

Central America
South America
West Indies
West Africa

Each tree annually produces anywhere from one to five pounds of precious cocoa beans, continuing to do so for a span of thirty to forty years. Thus a generous tree may yield as many as eighty thousand beans during its existence.

Cocoa beans come in many varieties, but can generally be classified as belonging to one of three types. *Criollo* is grown only in Central and South America, and is referred to as "the prince of cacaos," in tribute to its delicious mild aroma, light color, and soft outer husk. Unfortunately, the *criollo* tree is especially fragile and susceptible to disease, thus its yield is quite small. Since *criollo* beans generally make up only about ten percent of the world crop, their use is restricted to the finest quality chocolate, or for blending, to lend their aristocratic flavor to a lesser type of cocoa bean.

Forastero cocoa is hardier, easier to cultivate, and far more plentiful. Its pods are thicker, its aroma stronger, and its flavor correspondingly harsher. *Forastero* trees are grown primarily in West Africa, and make up the great majority of the world cacao crop.

Trinitario, the third type of cocoa bean, contains hybrids of the first two types. Its characteristics fall somewhere between the other two types.

Whatever the type of cocoa bean, harvesting procedures are basically the same. Harvest time occurs twice a year, in May and October or November. Because of the cacao tree's delicate nature, harvesting the cocoa beans is always a particularly tricky proposition. The trees cannot

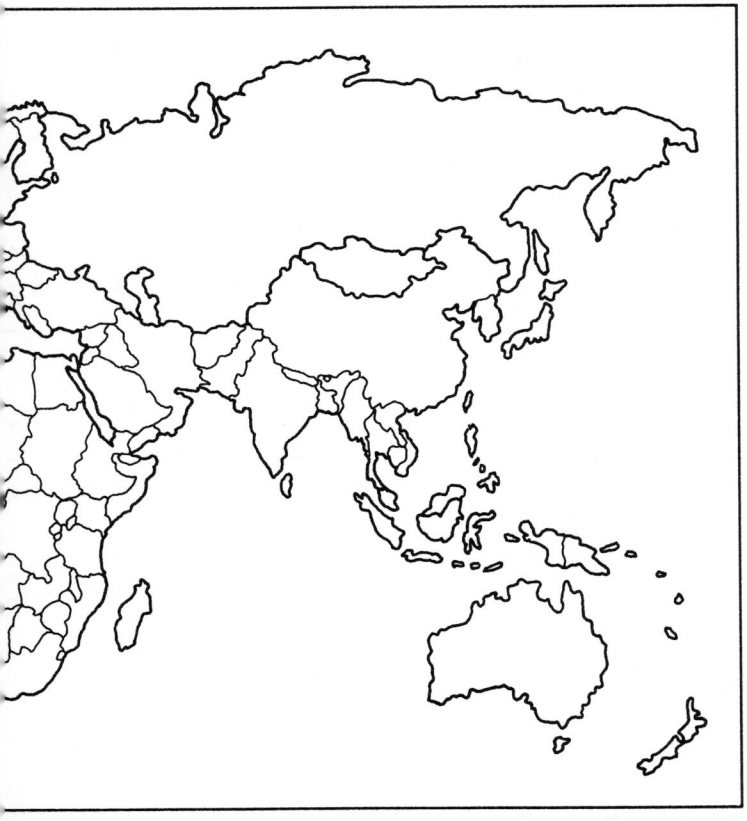

support a person's weight, so workers are unable to climb up and reach the higher pods. Instead, they use large steel knives attached to poles to get at the high pods, and machetes to cut down those pods within reach.

Gatherers then collect the pods in baskets, amassing huge piles. Machetes are used again to split open the shells (an experienced opener can split five hundred pods per hour) and extract both the cocoa beans and the pulp that surrounds them.

When the beans are first scooped out, they are beige in color, but after exposure to air they take on a purplish hue. The beans then undergo the critical process of fermentation, which takes from two to nine days depending on the variety of bean involved. Fermentation is necessary to remove the bitterness from both the beans' fragrance and flavor. In this process, the beans are heaped together (either on the ground or in boxes or baskets), covered with banana or plantain leaves or palm fronds, and turned several times to ensure an even fermentation. The bacteria in the beans ferments the sugar in their pulp, while surplus moisture drains out and evaporates. During this time the beans' temperatures may increase up to 125 degrees Fahrenheit, killing their germinating capabilities and unleashing enzymes. These enzymes are responsible for certain key chemical reactions that succeed in counteracting bitterness and fostering future flavor. At the end of the fermentation period, the beans have at last turned brown.

Drying is the next step. The beans are spread out on bamboo mats or on the ground for a particularly important sunbath. It may take from several days to a week for the beans to lose their moisture. During this time, they are also turned and picked over for defects or extraneous matter, such as pebbles. When drying is complete, the beans have been reduced to almost half their original weight, and have taken on an even deeper brown color and a more richly aromatic fragrance. Finally, the beans are weighed, classified, and packed into jute sacks. They have graduated from their botanic preparatory school and are ready to enter the institution of higher refinement—the chocolate factory.

MANUFACTURE

WHEN THE COCOA BEANS ARRIVE AT THEIR NEW HOME, THE CHOCOLATE FACTORY, they must be stored carefully in order not to absorb any odors or otherwise deteriorate in quality. They are placed in well-ventilated silos or warehouses in an environment where both temperature and humidity can be precisely regulated.

The beans are cleaned, sorted, and blended prior to roasting, which is done in large rotary cylinders or in an automatic conveyor belt system, in a manner similar to that used with coffee beans. The roasting process takes from half an hour to two hours in the cylinders, or from fifteen to twenty minutes by conveyor, at temperatures of over 250 degrees Fahrenheit. During roasting, the beans become a still darker brown and take on a familiar, evocative "chocolate" aroma.

After the beans are cooled, their shells, which have become brittle during roasting, can be removed readily. The beans are placed in the crushing machine, where they are broken into smaller pieces and separated from their husks, leaving the cocoa meat or "nibs." The crushed nibs are then weighed and blended prior to grinding.

First the nibs are preground in mills, which still leaves them somewhat coarse and gritty. From there, rollers grind them into a fine paste. This process generates an intense heat, which melts the cocoa butter (a fatty substance comprising about half of each nib), creating an aromatic, dark, thick liquid that is known as "chocolate liquor" (a nonalcoholic substance not to be confused with that ultimate nightcap, chocolate liqueur).

Part of this chocolate liquor is then put through a hydraulic press to extract the cocoa butter. The remaining chocolate liquor is blended and refined. Later, during the preparation of eating chocolate, some of the cocoa butter will be put back into it. (Plain chocolate liquor can also be molded into blocks, cooled, and sold as unsweetened baking chocolate for use by confectioners or home bakers.)

When the cocoa butter is removed from the press, what remains are cocoa cakes, which after being crushed, ground and sifted, become cocoa powder. This is the same cocoa powder used by professional bakers and confectioners. When sugar is added to it, cocoa powder becomes the basis for our own hot chocolate: the modern-day version of *chocolatl*.

As mentioned earlier, to make the chocolate we eat, cocoa butter must be added to chocolate liquor. When these two basic ingredients are combined with sugar, *voilà*, plain dark chocolate is made. When milk is also added, the result is milk chocolate. So-called "white" chocolate (which many do not consider true chocolate because it contains no chocolate liquor) consists simply of cocoa butter, sugar, and milk.

When these ingredients (plus flavorings such as the trusty vanilla) are combined to create various types of eating chocolate, they are first put into a mixing machine, where they are blended to form a doughy, still gritty substance. At this stage the combination tastes good, but it is not particularly smooth. True chocolate lovers might be sorely tempted to dig into the appetizing goo and help themselves, but this is comparable to eating raw cookie batter—far better to wait a few more steps. The mixture is then ground through heavy rollers, which smooth it further. However, the concoction must still undergo more refining through the conching process. This involves placing the chocolate into large troughs where it is heated and treated with rollers, which pass through it continually for two, three, or sometimes more days. At the end of this process, the chocolate is smooth enough to actually melt on the tongue. The chocolate is then tempered, or cooled from a hot liquid mass into a substance that is cool enough to be poured into molds or shaped.

In order to make the humble chocolate bar, for example, the cooled liquid chocolate is put through a pouring machine. The machine pours uniform amounts of chocolate into molds, which pass by on conveyor belts. The filled molds are then brought to the "shaking line," where they are vibrated and shaken so that the chocolate spreads out properly and air bubbles are removed. The molds then reach the cooling tower, where the chocolate solidifies. At this point, the molds are turned upside down and shaken, which dislodges the chocolate bars. The bars then proceed to wrapping machines, after which they reach the stores, our pockets, and eventually, our mouths!

Chocolate bars containing nuts, raisins, or other ingredients are made exactly as just explained, except that these extra ingredients are blended with the cooled liquid chocolate before it is poured.

Filled chocolate bars require a bit more work. As soon as the chocolate is poured into molds, the molds are turned over so that some of the chocolate falls out, while leaving a thin coating on the inside surfaces of the molds. This coating is then cooled and hardened. The molds are turned right side up again, and various fillings are poured in and cooled. More liquid chocolate is poured on top of the filling, and the bars are cooled once again. Later, the molds are inverted and the filled chocolate bars emerge triumphant.

Individual chocolates and filled chocolates are made in the factory in three different ways. The first procedure resembles that used to make filled chocolate bars, in which assorted soft or liquid fillings are poured into molds lined with chocolate, then covered with an additional layer of chocolate. The second operation involves hard centers being placed on a conveyor belt and brought to a coating machine, which coats them with chocolate. The third process involves pouring liquid chocolate into molds and centrifuging it so that it spreads evenly. This forms the shell for bonbons and truffles. The shells are then filled with various delights, which are injected by machine into a small opening, cooled, and finally sealed with a bit of liquid chocolate, surely the best glue ever invented.

Perhaps you are still wondering how chocolate figures—such as the venerable Easter rabbit—are made. These, too, require special molds. Your solid bunny (the only kind worth giving, in this writer's humble opinion) is composed of two corresponding molded halves, which are warmed and pressed together so they adhere to each other. For hollow chocolate figures (which deceive the eyes, deflate the palate, and depress

Chocolate Molds

In chocolate parlance, the word "mold" carries only the best of connotations. As more and more chocolate lovers turn to home chocolate making, they are looking beyond the traditional bunnies and eggs, and seeking out interestingly-shaped molds to give their chocolates that special look. These days, one can find molds with more personal trademarks, such as grand pianos, Volkswagens, telephones, racquetball racquets, and airplanes— not to mention such perennial favorites as hearts, teddy bears, turkeys, and Santas.

Molds are available in plastic and metal. The metal variety are heavier and more expensive, but they gener-

Nutritional Information

Read on if you need hard facts to encourage you to indulge. We have already established that chocolate, in moderation, can actually be beneficial to one's diet. But if you need further ammunition to convince others of that fact, or if you would simply like additional justification for eating an extra bar now and then, there is some information that should help. The following equivalencies show how surprisingly well chocolate stacks up against other not-nearly-so-tasty alternatives.

Using United States Department of Agriculture statistics, the Chocolate Manufacturers Association of America has determined that one plain milk chocolate bar has more protein than can be found in a banana, an apple, a package of seedless raisins, an orange, or a carrot.

This same bar also has more vitamin A than a package of seedless raisins, six peanut butter and cheese sandwich crackers, or one ounce of almonds.

ally yield better results than their plastic counterparts. You might want to try working with some inexpensive plastic molds first, to see if they work well for you, before you invest in the metal variety. However, if you are interested in display as well as use, the attractive metal molds (some of which are bona fide antiques) might be just the thing to dress up your kitchen.

Chocolate molds are becoming widely available. Try local candy or gourmet food shops for the basic shapes. If you like to hunt for antiques, ask your favorite sources to keep an eye out for unusual one-of-a-kind molds. Chocolate molds can also be ordered by mail from suppliers, who stock a wide variety of interesting shapes: Maid of Scandinavia, Madame Chocolate, Allmetal Chocolate Mold Co., Inc., and the Chocolate Mailbox.

It has more riboflavin than the banana, apple, carrot, orange, raisins, or peanut butter and cheese sandwich crackers.

The milk chocolate bar bests its competition in calcium content, coming out ahead of the banana, apple, orange, carrot, raisins, almonds, and peanut butter and cheese crackers.

It also does well in iron content, topping the apple, the orange, the carrot, and the crackers.

And when it comes to carbohydrates, which nutritionists now stress as being vital to a well-balanced diet, the milk chocolate bar beats the orange, the carrot, the crackers, and the almonds.

As for fats, which are also essential, who else but the chocolate bar reigns supreme over the banana, apple, orange, carrot, raisins, and, of course, crackers?

So, for the puritans among us who need an excuse to treat themselves, forget the taste, the texture, the aroma of chocolate. Just grit your teeth, and force yourself to swallow. Remember, it's for your own good.

Types of Couverture

The sophisticated chocolate lover knows that "couverture," or coating chocolate (also called "bulk chocolate"), is often chocolate at its best. This chocolate, favored by professional chocolatiers and chefs, and used by the cognoscenti for all their chocolate creations, contains extra cocoa butter and thus is shinier, softer, and imparts a smoother-looking, more desirable surface than regular chocolate.

Because it is primarily intended for professional use, couverture is usually sold in large quantities. However, you may be able to order your own supply directly from manufacturers, who may be persuaded to sell you a smaller than usual amount. Of course, you could always order the large amount, taking advantage of the keeping properties of chocolate.

Among the favored types of couverture available are Callebaut white, milk, bittersweet, and semisweet, available from Chocolaterie Bernard Callebaut in Toronto. "Nestlé Unsweetened Chocolate for Baking" and "Snowcap" (white chocolate), can be ordered from The Chocolate Collection from Nestlé; they only ship in the continental United States. Also good are Guittard, available from Guittard Chocolate Co. in the United States and from I.F.F. Sales, Pacific Candy, Oliver's Candies, Morden, Cakery Decor, Cheminee au Chocolat, Gale's Wholesale, H and D Hobby Distributors, and Hickory Farms in Canada. You might also try Merckens; from Merckens Chocolate Co.

the heart), liquid chocolate is centrifuged as in the third process for individual chocolates. The end product is an empty shell, albeit of chocolate, which teaches the futility of splitting hares.

CREATION OF CHOCOLATE

THE EXPLANATION OF CHOCOLATE MAKING IN THE "MANUFACTURE" SECTION describes what goes on in some of the most streamlined and sophisticated chocolate factories around the world. Such efficiency and organization can lead to the banal, if not profane, chocolates that come out of

Evolution of Praline

Today, the term "praline" has two different, equally delectable, meanings. To the Europeans, praline (pronounced "prah-lee-neh") refers to individual pieces of fine chocolate of all varieties. But praline (ironically pronounced "pray-lean") also refers to a specific confection—a popular filling prepared from finely ground almonds or hazelnuts and sugar. Praline is favored by many who like a nutty flavor without an overt aggressive crunch.

How did pralines get their name? It seems that in 1671, the French Duke of Plessis-Praslin, a famous gourmet, awaited his dessert one evening. Meanwhile, in the kitchen, a kitchen boy awkwardly dropped a bowl of almonds on the floor. The chef, while scolding him, spilled a pan of hot, burnt, caramelized sugar on top of the almonds. Having ruined his ingredients, the desperate chef served the unorthodox sugar-coated almonds to the Duke, who liked the new combo so much that he immediately lent his own name, "Praslin," to it. The rest, as they say, is history.

vending machines and are sold at your local corner candy store—or the result may be superb chocolates, particularly from Switzerland and Italy, where the techniques of chocolate factories are at their most advanced.

However, there is another way to make chocolates. Just as many gourmet cooks are going back to classic recipes and abandoning such ultramodern conveniences as microwaves and food processors for slower ovens and the mortar and pestle, so too are chocolate makers practicing their art in the classic manner. Some of the best chocolatiers are buying their own cocoa beans, which they roast, blend, conch, and temper themselves, in small, lovingly prepared batches. Others prefer to start with their favorite variety or blends of "couverture," bittersweet block chocolate with extra cocoa butter added, which must still be tempered. Being able to choose—and mix—couvertures helps the gourmet chef produce a chocolate basis onto which, depending on other ingredients and molds used, an individual can place his or her own stamp.

In fact, true luxury chocolates are often (but by all means not always) those made not in huge factories but in smaller candy kitchens, and in smaller amounts. They are sometimes hand-molded and hand-dipped. They always make use of the finest ingredients and eschew preservatives. These special chocolatiers take the fewest shortcuts and spend the most time on each morsel. The molds used are antique, or else unique. Naturally, the end result costs more—sometimes quite a bit more. Yet even at the pinnacle of chocolate perfection, you won't need a Swiss bank account to indulge.

What to Look for in a Chocolate

YOU PROBABLY ALREADY HAVE YOUR FAVORITE CHOCOLATE MANUFACTURER, EVEN the particular piece of chocolate you most prefer. But it is time to expand your chocolate horizons. With prices now as high as twenty-five and thirty dollars per pound, though, how do you ensure that the chocolate you are buying is high-quality, not just hype? Following are some characteristics of fine chocolate to look for the next time you decide you are ready to move up a rung on the chocolate ladder.

First of all, look at the chocolate. It should be shiny, an indication that sufficient cocoa butter has been used in its preparation. A dull finish indicates that artificial fats were probably used as substitutes, in order to save money. Cocoa butter has a unique way of combining with chocolate liquor to impart a special melt-on-the-tongue sensation that cannot be duplicated.

Any "quality" chocolate that is not shiny, but instead evinces a whitish or grayish cast, should immediately be rejected, no matter how exalted its pedigree. Such chocolate has "bloomed," a pretty name for an ignominious condition. Regardless of how glorious this chocolate once was, it is now well past its prime. This is a particular consideration to keep in mind when purchasing imported chocolates. Although Herculean efforts are usually made to ensure that delicate, preservative-free chocolates arrive at their final destination in peak form, accidents do happen, especially in less than ideal climate conditions.

When sampling a piece of chocolate, try to wait a bit before you blithely pop the entire morsel into your mouth. Instead, first place it in your hand. Fine chocolate will feel cool—due to its cocoa butter content—and will begin to melt when it comes into contact with your body heat. (Naturally, there's nothing wrong with licking your fingers for such a noble cause.) Contrary to that old advertisement extolling the virtues of candy that did not melt in one's hand, this "chocolate mess" is actually a hallmark of better chocolates: cocoa butter melts a lot faster than sugar, so the chocolates with the most cocoa butter and the least sugar will melt first.

Your nose can also tell you a great deal about the quality of chocolate you are buying. Sniff a piece and see whether you like the aroma. Both too sweet and too bitter scents should be shunned. Another way to profit by your sense of smell is to open an entire box of chocolates and sniff. There should be a definite, pleasing chocolate aroma. If the strongest scent is that of the paper used to pack the bonbons, this should tell you to be wary about the quality of the chocolates inside.

When considering which chocolate bar to buy, first break it and examine the edges. Good chocolate will give you a clean, noncrumbly break. If the bar is thick and of high quality, you will actually hear a sharp snap when you break it. (Of course, marching into a shop and breaking open the chocolate bars will not make you too popular with the proprietor. The idea is to buy the bar first, try your experiment, then taste. The next time you're ready to buy, you'll know whether to reach for the same bar or have the fun of trying another.)

The next step in your buying odyssey should be to talk to a salesperson. Find out what kind of cocoa beans are used in the production of the chocolate. (Remember that South American beans, particularly those from Venezuela, are more desirable—and also rarer and more pricey than African beans.) Ask whether the chocolate contains any preservatives or artificial ingredients (both are definite no-no's when a lot of money is being spent). Also ask how much, if any, of the work involved in making the chocolate is done by hand. Always keep in mind that hand-dipped chocolates will not look as uniformly elegant as their machine-made counterparts. However, their slightly less predictable appearance should be viewed as evidence that each chocolate is unique, and made with loving human care and supervision.

Chocolate-Making Countries

FOR THOSE OF US FOR WHOM CHOCOLATE MAKES THE WORLD GO ROUND, THE WORLD of chocolate is ripe for exploration. Just as each country has its own distinctive styles of art, architecture, couture, and cuisine, so too do different nations produce chocolates with a certain recognizable national character. Luckily, there is no need to rate the following countries in terms of the quality of their chocolate. All are capable of producing superb examples of their own national chocolate style—as well as some surprising variations on a theme. Now that sophisticated packaging and rapid transport have made the world's chocolates so accessible, it is relatively simple to conduct your own around-the-world chocolate tour without leaving home. Following are some general guidelines on the chocolate styles of Belgium, Switzerland, France, the Netherlands, Italy, Germany, Great Britain, and the United States. You'll want to use these recommendations to start on your own personal chocolate odyssey.

BELGIUM

FOR MANY AN AFICIONADO, BELGIAN CHOCOLATE IS CONSIDERED THE MOST SOPHIS-ticated, the prettiest, the shiniest—in a word, the best. Known for its deep, dark flavor, its lighter-than-air crème fraîche and buttery praline fillings, and the intricacies of its molded pieces, Belgian chocolates are an adult's delight. These are the chocolates for lovers. Each piece should be slowly and completely savored to appreciate its beauty and complexity.

Belgian chocolate may also be the best choice for dieters, because you can be satisfied after eating only one or two exquisitely rich pieces. Unfortunately, though, the pieces tend to be *so* exquisite that the temptation to indulge in just one more can be overwhelming.

Examples of the best Belgian chocolates are Corné de la Toison d'Or, Manon, Neuhaus, d'Orsay, Leonidas, and Bruyerre.

SWITZERLAND

SWISS CHOCOLATES MELT DIVINELY IN THE MOUTH. THEY ARE SO SMOOTH, CREAMY, and fresh-tasting that to bite into them is to conjure up visions of sunny green meadows, gentle streams, wildflowers, and bright blue skies—a trip back to a time when innocence and honesty reigned supreme.

While many adore the Swiss chocolate bar, placing it above those of all other nations in terms of quality and variety, let us not forget the crowning achievement of Swiss chocolate making—the truffle. Somehow the Swiss have mastered the secret of the ethereal art of truffle making, and no other nation comes close to duplicating those meltingly magic morsels of chocolate, butter, and cream, extravagantly filled with champagne and other nectars of the gods.

All Swiss chocolates tend to be sparkling clean, beautifully packaged, and delightful to eat. If milk chocolate is a particular favorite of yours, the Swiss variety might just become your number one choice. The cows who live up in the Alps must be happy indeed with their bucolic existence, for the milk that finds its way into Swiss chocolate imparts a special flavor that is uniquely comforting and satisfying.

Examples of the best Swiss chocolates are Teuscher, Lindt, Moreau, Tobler, and Suchard.

FRANCE

FRANCE, THE NATION OF GOURMET CUISINE *PAR EXCELLENCE*, CUSTOMARILY HAS not been known for its chocolate. However, to dismiss French chocolate as inconsequential would be a grievous mistake. The best French chocolate can be superb: dense, dark, and aromatic, the kind of bittersweet experience best appreciated by adult palates.

Many French chocolates have a smoky, coffee-like undertaste and, indeed, are at their best when enjoyed along with a steaming cup of café filtre or a glass of cognac. As you might expect, French chocolates are attractive to look at and stylishly packaged, the perfect gift for your favorite gourmand.

Examples of the best French chocolate are Pierre Koenig, Fouquet, Michel Guérard (this French chef's chocolates are made in Belgium, but they are typically French in style), and Panel.

THE NETHERLANDS

DUTCH CHOCOLATE, WHILE PRACTICALLY SYNONYMOUS WITH THAT FRAGRANT steaming brew we look to for sustenance on the coldest winter days, is more than superlative cocoa. It is also delightful by the bar and by the piece.

The best Dutch chocolate is rich, smooth, and hearty—never bitter. It melts creamily on the tongue, inciting the taste buds of young and old alike to clamor for more. While the Dutch do not use the beautiful antique molds as do other European nations, their chocolate is attractive and pleasant looking in its simplicity. If your child has outgrown sugary domestic bars and is ready to try something better, start him or her on Dutch milk chocolate. It's everything the candy bar was meant to be— only better.

Examples of the best Dutch chocolate are Droste, Van Houten, and Driessen.

ITALY

ITALIAN CHOCOLATE? IT'S *BELLISSIMA*. IF YOU THINK ITALY CAN ONLY PRODUCE GREAT wine and pasta, wait till you discover their chocolate.

Italian chocolate shares the best characteristics of its European neighbors. It is smooth, subtle, and sophisticated, sweet without being cloying. And since the hazelnuts that make up both praline and *gianduja* come primarily from the northern Piedmont region, it stands to reason that Italian chocolates use these native treasures to the best—and most sublime—advantage.

Italian chocolates tend to be attractively made and extremely well presented. A special delight is the whimsical shaping of certain pieces. How appropriate that the country that perfected pasta has duplicated one of the most popular pasta shapes, ravioli, in delicious dark and milk chocolate.

Examples of the best Italian chocolate are Perugina, Pernigotti, and Motta.

GERMANY

GERMANY PRODUCES SOME OF THE WORLD'S DEEPEST, DARKEST, AND MOST delicious bittersweet chocolate. This is robust, flavorful stuff, not for the faint of palate.

German chocolate is also velvety smooth, almost unctuous. If you like your bittersweet chocolate to emphasize chocolate rather than sugar, you're bound to be pleased with the German variety. It can also be used with superior results in home baking, something to keep in mind when you're experimenting with the ultimate recipe for Black Forest cake or rich and memorable chocolate tortes.

Lastly, be sure to look for German chocolate–coated marzipan. This sugary almond delicacy, which the Germans seem to make better than anyone else, lends itself to being paired with contrastingly bittersweet German chocolate.

Examples of the best German chocolate are Sarotti, Sprengel, Reber, and Stork (an American chocolatier whose products are gloriously German).

UNITED KINGDOM

BRITISH CHOCOLATE TENDS TO BE SWEETER THAN THAT OF THE REST OF EUROPE. Yet sweetness does not have to mean insipidity. These chocolates are creamy and mellow, sweet but not too sugary.

British chocolate is at its best when paired with spicy, zesty ginger or other tasty fruits. And if you're fond of mints, look no further. The British work wonders when it comes to combining mint and bittersweet chocolate, for a refreshingly tongue-tingling after-dinner treat.

Among British chocolates one may also find the favorites of bygone days: candied violets and rose creams, for example. In fact, whatever

Whatever its nationality, chocolate abounds in a variety of natural forms. Shown above are some of the more unusually shaped delicacies in bite-size pieces.

chocolates you fancy will probably be found in the United Kingdom—from bittersweet truffles with rum centers to pristine vanilla creams.

Examples of the best chocolates the United Kingdom has to offer are Charbonnel et Walker, Fortnum and Masons, Joseph Terry, and J. & A. Ferguson.

UNITED STATES

AS BEFITS THIS MELTING POT, ONE CAN FIND CHOCOLATES OF EVERY DESCRIPTION, from every nation, being made in the United States. Thus America is the home of distinguished "continental" chocolates, as well as the simpler and equally delicious "homestyle" variety.

American chocolates are at their best when they don't put on airs, but make plentiful use of top-quality ingredients and are served in large quantities. Who could resist a chunk of crunchy, nutty almond buttercrunch, dripping with buttery milk chocolate, or a generous mouthful of chocolate caramel pecan "turtle"? And who else but an American could have been inspired to combine peanut butter with milk chocolate—surely a match made in chocolate lovers' heaven. Also in this down-to-earth category are good old-fashioned chocolate bars, thick and satisfyingly chewy, just made to be washed down with an ice-cold glass of milk.

Yet American chocolate is fast becoming more than childhood candy favorites, hot fudge sundaes, and chocolate chip cookies. As Americans gain sophistication as cooks and consumers of gourmet foods, so too have they turned to more grown-up types of chocolate. Skilled chefs are now creating a revolution in American chocolate. Leading the way are truffles that rival—and sometimes surpass—Europe's in their excellence. It is now possible to find American chocolates that are every bit as stylish as Belgian, and as smooth and creamy as Swiss. Yet, these special chocolates manage to maintain their American integrity and identity with more generous sizes and interesting, sometimes unlikely, combinations of ingredients. For American—and Canadian—chocoholics, right now is "the best of times." And the best of times will continue to get better and better.

Examples of the best American chocolate are Harbor Sweets, Dilettante, Wilbur, and any of the San Francisco "American-sized," European-style truffle makers.

Chocolatiers

AUSTRIA

HOFBAUER VIENNA, LTD.

"AUSTRIA'S FINEST," PROCLAIMS THE ELEGANT SCRIPT ON THE CHOCOLATE BROWN Hofbauer container, and indeed, these excellent bonbons live up to their promise. Hofbauer has been making chocolates since 1882, and in recognition of their superior quality, has been granted permission by the Austrian government to use the official Austrian crest on its packages.

You may be tempted to hum a few strains of a Viennese waltz when you bite into Hofbauer's *"Rohkost"* (mouthwatering orange peel, apricots, plums, dates, figs, or hazelnuts dipped into seductively dark chocolate) or as you savor Hofbauer's superior truffles, marzipan, and milk chocolate sandwiched around smooth hazelnut praline paste.

Hofbauer's packaging is charmingly old-world and *gemütlich*. Boxed assortments may have an elaborate petit point design, or they may depict gold-framed Viennese engravings or a photograph of the majestic Lippizaner stallions. These pretty boxes would do any grandmother's coffee table proud.

Appropriately, the Hofbauer motto is *in qualitate robur*, "in quality lies strength." Judging from the quality of these fine chocolates, the Hofbauer tradition is still going strong.

You can purchase Hofbauer chocolates at New York City's Bremen House or at local German specialty gourmet shops. Write or call Hofbauer for more information about where to find them near you.

BELGIUM

CHOCOLATERIE CORNÉ TOISON D'OR

CORNÉ IS A TRADITIONAL BELGIAN CHOCOLATIER WHOSE PROUD MOTTO, "NO OTHER shall I have," has been taken to heart by European chocolate fanciers for nearly fifty years. Now American and Canadian lovers of fine chocolates are also embracing Corné's superbly sophisticated chocolate collection.

Why the acclaim? First of all, Corné is that rarity, a firm perfectionist—even roasting its own cocoa beans. Using the finest obtainable South American beans, Corné blends to its own formulation and stringently controls the time and temperature crucial to the actual roasting process.

Thus, different beans are specially roasted and blended, so that each Corné chocolate is extremely distinct and utterly unique. The result is that Corné's plain chocolate has a lovely strong taste, redolent of the "smokiness" that is justly favored by connoisseurs.

As you might expect, a firm so particular about its beans would be equally adamant about using only the finest natural ingredients. Hence, Corné's crème fraîche, buttercream, and praline fillings are impeccably pedigreed and taste exquisite. And Corné also makes four different kinds of caramel, each delicious.

As for the molds used to form the chocolates, they, too, are special—both in appearance and detail. There is a sublime solid chocolate teddy bear, whose plaintive ursine expression and finely wrought fur render him irresistible—the ultimate chocolate lover's teddy. Another example of Corné's artistry is the *"Javanais,"* a dark chocolate ear of corn, correct down to the last kernel, whose filling consists of half mocha and half praline. The combination is inspired, and the piece itself is beautiful to behold. The *"Grappe,"* a dark chocolate cluster of grapes, complete with leaves at the top, is filled with orange cream containing tiny bits of orange. Its flavor is creamy and adult, chocolatey rather than sweet. Another noteworthy item is Corné's splendid chocolate truffle, which combines four different chocolates in one mouth-watering piece. Making their presence felt are strong cocoa powder, a dark chocolate shell, creamy chocolate ganache, and lighter chocolate at the center. This truffle can easily hold its own among the best.

Corné's New York City outpost is that bastion of luxe, Fifth Avenue's Trump Tower. The shop is small and snug, gleaming with marble and glass and accented with fresh flowers. But its real highlight is the display case, which handsomely presents each chocolate over a label giving both the name of the piece and a description of its contents—helpful for those who like to know what's inside every piece (before they select, or bite into, it).

Non-New Yorkers need not despair of getting their share of Corné's treats. There is a Corné shop in Montreal, with plans for more now in the works. The chocolates are also available in outlets such as Bloomingdale's, Magnin's in San Francisco, Rich's in Atlanta, Creeds in Canada, Willis Furniture in Norfolk, Virginia, Piret's in San Diego, and By Design in Los Angeles, among others.

Corné will fill mail orders, except during the warm weather period between Memorial Day and Labor Day. So, if you, too, are a convert to their "no other shall I have" motto, Corné can probably satisfy your own chocolate cravings regardless of where you live.

CHOCOLATERIE GALLER

THESE DELICIOUS BELGIAN CHOCOLATE BARS ARE SO TASTY AND ELEGANT, THEY should bear the legend, "For adults only." It takes a well-educated palate to appreciate the superb *"Brésilia,"* whose deep dark chocolate exterior shelters an aromatic coffee cream filling; the *"Blanc de Coco,"* with its ultrasmooth white chocolate exterior filled with coconut-flecked, hazelnut-flavored chocolate (a favorite at the famed Cesar's Palace Hotel); and the lovely *"Blanc de Praliné,"* in which the aforementioned buttery white chocolate is filled with a delightful crunchy hazelnut paste.

Galler also makes a delicious *pâte au chocolat*, literally, chocolate paste, which can be spread on cakes or cookies, or can be used European-style to create a chocolate sandwich that is destined to be a chocolate devotee's favorite snack.

Galler chocolates are available in New York at Dean and DeLuca's, DDL Foodshow, Balducci's, and Macy's; by mail order through Madame Chocolate of Glenview, IL; through importer Marique Enterprises Ltd. for the location nearest you in the United States; or through Godon Closet for Canada.

CHOCOLATERIE BRUYERRE

THE PEOPLE AT BRUYERRE LIKE TO THINK OF THEMSELVES NOT AS A CHOCOLATE manufacturer, but as a chocolate kitchen, in which old favorite recipes are lovingly recreated. Rather than become a high-volume business, they prefer to maintain their reputation for high quality with thirty-seven special pieces of chocolate. Sadly, due to their alcohol content, only twenty-one of these pieces can be exported to the United States; but twenty-one out of thirty-seven isn't bad!

Handcraftsmanship is a large part of Bruyerre's charm. It is strikingly evident in the *"Corbeille,"* a delicate molded milk chocolate basket the bottom level of which is filled with a core of hazelnut paste, topped with a swirling mixture of hazelnuts, milk chocolate, and whipping cream, then fastened with a tiny golden handle.

Other lovely pieces are the *"Giandale,"* in which a milk chocolate shell dusted with sugar and swirled with special forks houses a smooth ganache of milk chocolate, whipping cream, and Cointreau liqueur; the *"Chantilly,"* a small white chocolate mountain hiding a filling of creamy beige mocha ganache; and the tower-shaped *"Millenaire,"* filled with hazelnut paste, mocha ganache, and a spalsh of Cointreau—created in 1980 to mark the thousand-year anniversary of Bruyerre's home, the city of Gosselies.

Bruyerre chocolates are typically Belgian in their richness of flavor and sophisticated design. Each piece is a complex blend of tastes, made to be savored slowly and appreciatively.

Bruyerre is available in New York City at Winter's Chocolatier and at Macy's Cellar. Contact Macy's if you want additional information concerning mail orders in North America.

LE CHOCOLATIER MANON

POSSIBLY THE MOST BEAUTIFUL CHOCOLATE SHOP IN ALL OF NEW YORK CITY, MANON is furnished with elegant antiques. There are tapestries on the wall, a rich burgundy carpet underfoot, a Venetian glass chandelier sparkling above, and a lavish assortment of fresh flowers, porcelains, and baskets. The effect is that of entering the private sitting room of a very fine lady. But the splendid display case that is the room's focal point leaves no doubt as to what you have come here for: sumptuous chocolates as only the Belgians can make them.

What makes Manon chocolates, flown in weekly by Sabena in a special air-cooled unit, so terrific? For one thing, the antique molds used to create one-of-a-kind pieces: strawberries with real dimples, children's heads, leaves, fans, flowers, and more. For another, the preponderance of crème fraîche, that richest and most delicate of fillings that no other nation seems capable of creating with such finesse. (The name *Manon*, in fact, is a reference to the legendary dairy maid Manon Lescaut.) At Manon it is not unusual to find two different kinds of crème fraîche, or two other contrasting types of filling, in an individual piece. This leads to an exquisiteness of taste combinations that is truly unique.

Examples of Manon's artistry abound: There is the *"Sputnik"*—shaped like a tiny space capsule of bittersweet chocolate, tipped in real gold. (Yes, you can eat the gold part, too!) The filling is an out-of-this-world combination of crème fraîche and orange. The *"Bouchon,"* or cork, is a bittersweet chocolate cup filled with a layer of chocolate buttercream topped with snowy crème fraîche. The *"Serpentin"* is pinecone-shaped milk- and dark-chocolate filled with praline cream, while the *"Milenka"* is filled with buttery, sinfully runny caramel whose texture is pure silk. A mouthwatering curiosity, the *"Enfant de Bruxelles"* is a piece shaped like a child's head (complete with curly hair) and filled with a combination of chocolate- and coffee-flavored crème fraîche. These are chocolates to savor. Enjoy their beauty as well as their taste, and you will begin to know true chocolate luxury.

Even Manon's packaging is superb: a burgundy bag with gold lettering, filled with pumpkin-colored tissue paper, and accented with a jaunty pumpkin-colored tassel. No ditsy pastels for these bold, full-bodied chocolates!

Although Manon is only available ouside of Brussels in two small New York City shops—one on the Upper East Side, and one in the Trump Tower—they will be glad to ship their chocolates (in the United States only) but not during the summer months. However, thick-bottomed pieces, such as the *"Escargot,"* a snail shell–shaped chocolate filled with runny praline cream, may arrive in good condition when the weather is warm. Contact the shop and ask their advice on what to order.

LEONIDAS/D'ORSAY

THIS TEAM OF TWO FINE BELGIAN CHOCOLATIERS IS WELL-NIGH INVINCIBLE. Leonidas, Belgium's largest chocolate producer (with 280 shops) and maker of the largest selling, most popular chocolate in a nation of chocolate lovers, has joined forces with d'Orsay, a very small workshop whose chocolates are all hand produced. The benefits of this merger accrue to the consumer.

Both companies' superlative chocolates are preservative free, and arrive fresh in the United States each week. Because they cannot be made with alcohol, as is customarily done in Belgium, Leonidas has acquired ultra-efficient new machinery to perform the specialized function of remaking the centers to acceptable (and delicious) United States formulations. D'Orsay, by contrast, still makes their chocolates by hand, as they have been doing for the past three hundred years. Their special couverture is so thick and rich that it cannot be machine processed.

Among the highlights of Leonidas chocolates are the *"White Manon,"* a large white chocolate crème fraîche piece—cool and delightful with its light and silky center of hazelnut praline and coffee, and the *"Merveilleux Molded,"* a milk chocolate exterior filled with luscious milk chocolate–flavored caramel.

D'Orsay's special pieces include the *"Rembrandt,"* a masterpiece of dark chocolate embossed with the image of the old master and filled with a unique mixture of praline and puffed rice; a milk chocolate *"Windmill,"* filled with orange peel ganache; and the *"Désiré,"* a swirl of chocolate praline filled with a lusty glazed cherry. D'Orsay also makes delectable buttery truffles in chocolate, coffee, vanilla, and praline flavors.

D'Orsay and Leonidas chocolates are available in New York City at DDL Foodshow and Faye and Allen's Foodworks, and in Florida at Belk's; plans are under way for Canadian distribution as well. Contact Pink Imports, Inc. for information regarding the location nearest you.

MICHEL GUÉRARD CHOCOLAT

AS BEFITS ANYTHING BEARING THE DISTINGUISHED NAME OF THIS CELEBRATED French chef, Michel Guérard chocolates are very special indeed. Not only are they lovely to look at, but they are also a pleasure to eat.

Guérard has created a chocolate that is extremely finely milled. This process results in chocolate with an exceptionally smooth texture, yet still capable of retaining its shape. Because of this technique, the chocolate is actually lighter—it takes fourteen chocolate leaves to make up one ounce!

Appropriately for a master of cuisine minceur, Guérard uses twenty-five percent less sugar than is customary in chocolate making. This allows the taste of the chocolate itself to shine through. (And no, this doesn't at all mean bitter-tasting chocolates.) After sampling these, you're apt to wonder why other manufacturers use so much sugar.

Although chef Guérard himself designed these delicious chocolates, they are produced in Brugge, outside Brussels, by fourth-generation chocolatiers. But Guérard still does oversee the process, touring the factory at least once a year.

While Guérard's chocolates are all of very high quality, several pieces are standouts. The aforementioned slender leaves, filled with ambrosial crème fraîche or sprightly mint crème fraîche, are marvelous both in their delicacy and their flavor. The cameo piece, which uses three types of chocolate—milk, dark, and white—to create a cameo image as precise as that of the real jewel, is both visually and culinarily pleasing. And the raspberry truffle, with its deep dark coating and splendid filling, succeeds nobly in capturing the essence of puréed raspberry without being distractingly tart or simperingly sweet. (Unfortunately, this truffle is rolled in granulated sugar—a needless excess, but one that can and should be overlooked given the other superb qualities present here.)

Michel Guérard's boxed chocolates, as well as a selection of his cooking chocolate and special molds, complete with directions for the ambitious home chef, are widely available in such upscale department stores as Neiman Marcus, Bloomingdale's, Macy's, Robinson's, and Burdine's, as well as at Eaton's and Simpson's in Canada.

NANOU CHOCOLAT

THIS FINE BELGIAN CHOCOLATE IS HANDMADE BY THE VANDERKERKEN FAMILY, WHO are no strangers to gourmet chocolate (a son owns the renowned Manon Chocolaterie in New York). Only first-quality ingredients are used: Callebaut couverture, dairy butter, fresh cream, and fresh eggs. Each delicate piece is lovely, with its own complex and satisfying taste. Among the best are dark and milk chocolates with crème fraîche centers that tickle the taste buds, dissolving gently on the tongue. Also memorable is the dark chocolate piece filled with cognac-flavored buttercream—a combination that is understated rather than distractingly sweet—and dark chocolate with *croquant* (crunchy caramel) filling, which provides not only taste but texture. Nanou makes fifteen praline paste pieces and seven different truffles, all of which are elegant, attractive, and tasty.

Nanou chocolates are available through Mme Larcele in Minneapolis, and in Beverly Hills' Chocolat du Monde. They will mail order throughout Canada and the United States.

NEUHAUS (U.S.A.) INC.

EXQUISITE NEUHAUS CHOCOLATES EXEMPLIFY THE BEST QUALITIES OF BELGIAN chocolate making. The company is world famous for its celebrated crème fraîche filling, and for the originality of its presentation. Each piece, beautifully molded, houses a wonderfully inventive filling.

CHOCOLATIERS

Mme Larcele

This delightful shop in Minneapolis' historic St. Anthony Main renovated district, on the banks of the Mississippi River, has been cited for its design excellence. Chocolate fans will cite it for its superior selection of chocolates as well. Mme Larcele carries four different lines of imported chocolates: Swiss, French, and Belgian chocolates under the store's own label, plus Belgian Nanou Chocolates, as well as domestic chocolates made especially for the shop.

The selection includes delicate Belgian fresh creams; exotic burnt caramel pieces; excellent smooth-textured dark and milk chocolate with such fillings as mocha and toffee; and charming French chocolate in the shape of provincial characters, zoo animals, and seashells. Mme Larcele also stocks a fine assortment of truffles from Belgium and from Kansas City's André Bollier, who has created a sparkling new champagne truffle exclusively for this store.

Customers may purchase these chocolates by the piece, in assortments, or by the pound. Mme Larcele also sells its chocolates wholesale to retailers around the United States, so it may be possible to encounter them at your favorite local chocolatier outside of the Twin Cities. They also are happy to accept mail and phone orders for delivery to the United States and Canada.

It is difficult to single out the best pieces from among so many worthy candidates, but deserving of distinction are the *"Pharaoh,"* an opulently bittersweet molded chocolate pharaoh filled with a neatly contrasting white nougat and chopped almond praline; the spicy Benedictine cream-filled dark chocolate horseshoe; the "125," dark chocolate filled with an unexpectedly flavorful pear nectar cream; and the chestnut cream-filled milk chocolate leaf called the *"Automne."*

Among the crème fraîche pieces, standouts are the milk chocolate toffee *"Tentation,"* filled with coffee crème fraîche; the simple yet majestic crème fraîche and chocolate powdered truffles rolled in cocoa powder; and the *"Vanilla,"* a smooth white chocolate piece containing crème fraîche, vanilla, and the welcome surprise of a whole walnut. And if all this is not enough, Neuhaus also produces *"Fruits de Mer,"* beautiful variegated white chocolate seashells filled with hazelnut praline, as well as filled chocolate hearts and eggs.

45

Neuhaus chocolates are available at major quality department stores, such as Macy's and Saks Fifth Avenue, and in gourmet and confectionery shops. In addition, there are four shops with the Neuhaus name: in Dallas at the Galleria and the Northpark Mall; in Costa Mesa, CA; and in Charleston, SC. Two more Neuhaus shops are planned for Hilton Head Island and Miami. In Montreal and Toronto, Neuhaus chocolates imported from Brussels are available at Holt Renfrew.

WINTERS CHOCOLATIER

WINTERS CARRIES OVER SIXTY DIFFERENT VARIETIES OF CHOCOLATE FROM SUCH respected Belgian chocolatiers as Neuhaus, Bruyerre, and Theo Brommer. All appear here under the Winters label. These are excellent chocolates, handmade with pure ingredients. All are without preservatives, and all possess that special elegance that sets apart Belgium's best from the competition.

Among the highlights of Winters's well-chosen collection is the *"Talère,"* a marbled milk and white chocolate exterior protecting a cream ganache with rum. Its taste is reminiscent of vanilla; the texture is vaguely mousselike. The *"Poulet,"* or "hen," aptly contains an egg liqueur buttercream. Surely an eggnog lover's delight, the piece is a fabulous combination of buttery soft chocolate in a hard dark chocolate shell. The *"Café Crème,"* or "coffee cream," has a subtle but distinctive coffee taste. The *"Amour"* is an appealing piece of chocolate filled with spicy vanilla buttercream and topped with a crunchy walnut.

Winters' "Chocolate Menu," listing pieces by number, name, and brief description, is a clever and useful innovation. Chocolate-craving consumers can read the menu until their appetite is properly whetted, and order by telephone 24-hours-a-day such exotica as the *"Pays d'Azur"* (praline with orange creme); *"Pistamande"* (pistachio marzipan), or *"L'Ananas"* (pineapple with fondant cream). Normally, the order will arrive anywhere where U.P.S. ships within two working days.

Those who visit the shop are in for a special treat—there is always a different piece of Belgian chocolate on the counter, for "consumer education"—in other words, a free sample for customers to try. When the chocolates are this imaginative and tasty, an educated consumer is truly the seller's best friend.

Alcohol in Chocolate

Although untutored American palates may crave a chocolate so sweet and grainy it practically cries out for a glass of milk to wash it down, Europeans are accustomed to a smoother, more sophisticated and flavorful chocolate. And if you ask a European chocolate aficionado what sets continental chocolates apart from their American counterparts, you'll probably get a one-word reply: alcohol.

It is essence of alcohol that elevates Swiss and Belgian chocolates from nursery status to their customary place of honor in the dining and drawing room. The judicious use of brandy, cognac, and other fine liqueurs imparts a special edge to European chocolates that cannot be duplicated solely by substituting "flavoring extracts" or artificial flavors. Yet residents of the United States (with the exception of three pioneers: Nevada, Kentucky, and Tennessee) are prohibited by law from savoring liquor- and liqueur-filled chocolates, except when traveling abroad.

According to the United States Federal Food and Drug Administration regulations, alcohol may not be used legally in candy at all, the only exception being the use of up to one-half of one percent by volume, if (and this is a big if) this alcohol is derived solely from the use of the aforementioned flavoring extracts.

As more European chocolate is imported into the United States, and more American chocolatiers continue to gain in technique, expertise, and sophistication, this prohibition is more strongly felt. There has been periodic agitation for a relaxation of FDA regulations, but at this writing, it appears that the revelation of biting into a chocolate-covered cherry cordial redolent with brandy or eau-de-vie is still a forbidden pleasure, denied even to consenting American adults.

For those connoisseurs lucky enough to live in Canada, the picture is somewhat less bleak. Canada has no federal restriction on this commodity, consequently many of Europe's best liqueur-filled chocolates can be found in specialty shops and some department stores.

CANADA

AU CHOCOLAT

IF TRUFFLES ARE YOUR PASSION, AU CHOCOLAT IS THE SHOP FOR YOU. THEY CARRY eleven luscious varieties of the sublime stuff, and for a mere dollar apiece you can experience nirvana. Among the favorites are a gorgeous Grand Marnier truffle, which proves once again that chocolate and oranges are made for one another, and a Cashew Truffle, which combines those terrific-tasting nuts with smoothly luxurious milk chocolate.

Should you get the urge to branch out beyond truffles, au Chocolat will provide you with delicious solid molded chocolate items as well. And if you can't get to au Chocolat, all is not lost—they will come to you. In book form, that is. Au Chocolat's book, *Oh Truffles*, provides recipes for the two truffles mentioned above, as well as such splendid offerings as the French Truffle (with crème fraîche), the Pure White Chocolate Truffle, and the Apricot Sacher Truffle (replete with apricot brandy and chopped dried apricots). The book can be ordered from Wilmor Publishing Corporation, c/o au Chocolat.

THE ULTIMATE TRUFFLE

SITUATED IN THE HISTORIC THORNHILL SECTION OF ONTARIO, JUST NORTH OF Toronto, The Ultimate Truffle is a mecca for Canadian chocolate lovers. The store itself is as quaint as its surroundings. The store's owner, a certified chef, attended the Confectionery School and Hotel Restaurant School in Holland. He has some old-fashioned ideas about chocolate-making as well. Only the finest imported chocolates and liqueurs are used in his truffles. The store carries 24 luscious varieties, including a sumptuous champagne raspberry creation, a Grand Marnier truffle, and their specialty cream truffles. All truffles are handmade daily.

The Ultimate Truffle also offers a pure chocolate truffle cake that is as delightful as you could imagine. The store will ship anywhere around the world for a standard price of $15 (Canadian) per pound, plus $2 for packing and postage. They will not, however, ship during June, July, and August for obvious reasons.

DENMARK

ANTHON BERG

CHOCOLATE LOVERS MAY NOT THINK OF DENMARK AS A SOURCE OF QUALITY CHOCO-late, but Anthon Berg has a creditable offering, with chocolates that have a smooth, pleasant, if unremarkable flavor. Among their most interesting offerings are the chocolate "Queen of Denmark" cordials, flavored with

Club Chocolat du Mois

The passing of each month becomes cause for celebration when you enroll yourself or a favored friend in "Club Chocolat du Mois," the chocolate of the month club. Membership can be purchased for three, five, eight, or the full twelve months of the year, and it entitles the member to a continuing delicious stash of high-quality, beautifully packaged chocolate.

Among the treats that come to your door are exclusives from the cream of California's truffle crop, represented by Lisa Lerner, the San Francisco Chocolate Company, and Chocolates from Chocolates. Also on tap are international chocolate favorites: French Pierre Koenig, Belgian Gudrun, and Swiss Moreau. During July, when it's usually too hot to ship chocolates, members receive an assortment of Grand Finale chocolate sauces in such flavors as Chocolate Fudge and Grand Marnier Chocolate Caramel. Nor are chocolate cake lovers neglected. They receive Narsai's Chocolate Decadence cake in June, and a Narsai's surprise, "guaranteed to be deliciously decadent," in September.

Prices for this bounty vary, depending on the plan selected. The deluxe plan costs thirty dollars per month and includes fancy wrapping and more chocolate. The regular plan is eighteen dollars, and uses less elaborate wrapping and fewer chocolates. Membership is available in the United States and Canada, and all members are guaranteed both safe delivery of their chocolates and satisfaction with each offering.

To join the club, contact them at 1736 Stockton Street, San Francisco, CA 94133. Or telephone (415) 398-7002.

either raspberry or strawberry. (The tarter raspberry is slightly preferable to the less-complex strawberry.)

The attractive "yellow rose" box assortment contains hazelnut, almond, marzipan, and mint chocolates, among others.

Anthon Berg chocolates are available throughout North America in specialty or gourmet shops, or check with Morris Imports for a location near you. Some of the stores that carry the chocolates are The Bay, Eaton's, Macy's, and Marshall Field's.

FRANCE

FOUQUET

VIVE LES CHOCOLATS DELICIEUX! FOUQUET, THE ELEGANT FRENCH GOURMET SHOP, has been creating superb handmade chocolates for 150 years. Their recipes require three times more cocoa than is customarily used. The cocoa beans called for are always prime Venezuelan. Mademoiselle Monique Fouquet insures that the other ingredients that go into her chocolates are equally pedigreed: imported vanilla, almonds, and walnuts, top quality honey, and fruit flavors extracted from natural, specially selected fruits.

Such careful and expert supervision results in splendid chocolates. Among the best are the crunchy dark chocolate almond pralines, dark chocolate filled with nougat or buttery caramel, and rich yet delicate coffee, raspberry, orange, and vanilla creams.

Naturellement, presentation of these fine chocolates is stylish and attractive. All boxes are hand packed and some are even hand painted. Each is wrapped with a satin ribbon.

Fouquet chocolates are available in Fouquet's two Parisian shops; if you can't trot off to France just now, it might be worth contacting Fouquet for the name of a specialty shop near you where they may be found. You might ask at your local department store, too.

PANEL

UNTIL RECENTLY, PANEL CHOCOLATES WERE SOLD IN FRANCE UNDER THE LABEL "homemade." But that humble designation does not begin to do justice to these epicurean delights, which are at least as lavish and elegant as their better known competitors.

The Panel family began making chocolates three generations ago in Lyon, a city celebrated by gourmets as the gastronomic capital of the world. Following in that esteemed city's proud tradition, Pierre Panel personally chose the raw materials for his chocolate confections: *Criollo* cocoa beans from the West Indies, Central America, and Trinidad, which he blended with African *Forastero* beans, choice Spanish almonds, and the plum and apricot fruit pastes that are Lyonnais specialties. Panel nurtured the chocolate through its preparatory stages, always maintaining total control over each piece.

Today, Pierre's grandson Jean-Claude has taken up the mantle of "artisan chocolatier," following the dictates of the master and continuing to choose his raw materials and prepare his chocolates from the same family recipes. The results are a revelation. Panel's "Monte Cristo," a walnut cream ganache, is dark, smooth, and luxurious. It melts on the tongue, leaving behind memories of intense chocolate flavor rather than simple sweetness. Similarly, Panel's chocolate almond nougat piece, with its splendidly crunchy praline coating, is a marvel of good breeding, in which each ingredient enhances the others and the resulting whole is far tastier than the sum of its parts. Even its aroma is uniquely chocolate, pure and intoxicating in its freshness. Also delicious is Panel's *"Café"* piece, which blends dark chocolate and coffee into a seductively silken bittersweet partnership.

Panel Chocolates are now available in New York at Balducci's, as well as in Paris, Osaka, and Tokyo.

PIERRE KOENIG
⚬⚬⚬

YES, VIRGINIA, THERE IS A REAL PIERRE KOENIG, WHO STILL MAKES HIS OWN exquisite chocolates by hand, at the back of his establishment in Metz-Lorraine, one hundred miles east of Paris. This gentleman is so proud of his confections that many of them bear his initials—and indeed, these are chocolates that would instill pride in any *confiseur.*

When you bite into a Pierre Koenig bonbon, it seems to say "chocolate" with a capital *C.* Koenig's bittersweet chocolate is very pronounced, providing an intense chocolate flavor with coffee undertones that renders his truffles irresistible. Yet Koenig's white chocolate truffles, flavored with essences of pear, *mirabelle* (the plum from which the famous *mirabelle* brandy is made), and orange, and colored in beautiful pastel shades of green, blue, and orange with the appropriate vegetable dyes, are equally delicious—though meltingly delicate and completely different from their dark chocolate cousins. Koenig's *framboise* piece has an appealingly strong, almost sharp flavor, that complements rather than overpowers its bittersweet chocolate coating.

Pierre Koenig's chocolates can be found in Paris at Fauchon, the gourmet food emporium par excellence. In the United States, they are available at San Francisco's Confetti and Le Chocolatier, and at Encore Confiserie in Anchorage, AK. So far, they are not yet available in Canadian shops, but these stores will mail order to the provinces.

GERMANY

REBER KUGELN
⚬⚬⚬

IF THE NAME WOLFGANG AMADEUS MOZART ONLY BRINGS TO MIND HIS *JUPITER Symphony,* you haven't experienced Reber's out-of-this-world "Mozart Kugel," a commemorative confection of extraordinary taste. This exquisite and delectable combination of milk and dark chocolates, hazelnuts, nougat, and pistachio almond marzipan is a veritable symphony of harmonious flavors.

Packaged in a dainty white ballotin adorned with a red, gold, and white portrait of the composer who gave this delicacy its name, these chocolates are a deliciously imaginative tribute. Bite into one and marvel at the symmetry of toasty brown nougat encircled half in green and half in white. The green takes its color from real pistachio, not from artificial tints or additives. And the luxurious dark chocolate that covers it all is meltingly delicious—like music to one's mouth.

A tasty companion piece is the "Constanze," named for Mozart's wife, and delicious in its own right. Composed of nougat, croquant, and orange flavored almond marzipan coated with silky milk chocolate, it too merits applause.

Reber Mozart Kugeln, Constanze Kugeln, and other tasty opuses are sold during New York City's "Mostly Mozart Festival," which takes place each summer at Avery Fisher Hall, as well as in better chocolate and delicatessen shops throughout North America. Americans should write to importer George C. Brown for the location nearest them. Canadians should direct their inquiries to David Ashley.

SAROTTI

DARK, RICH, AND INTENSELY FLAVORFUL, SAROTTI CHOCOLATES ARE THE PRODUCT of a Germany company owned by Nestlé, and produced in a new, modern Berlin factory. Sarotti *"Edel Bitter"* has a deep chocolate taste that is unique. This smooth bitter chocolate melts on the tongue, leaving behind memories of the essence of chocolate so strong it tastes almost like coffee. Sarotti's bar of milk chocolate with a smooth hazelnut center is sleekly creamy and light tasting, a fine companion to the more assertive *Edel Bitter*.

Sarotti's dark chocolate bonbons filled with Napoleon brandy are a revelation. The pity is that their alcohol content makes them *verboten* in the United States. But other Sarotti assortments are available here, and they are tasty enough to be worth a search. In Canada, contact your provincial Liquor Commissioner for information on regulations governing the sale of liquor-filled chocolates.

Sarotti bar and boxed chocolates have always been delicious, top-of-the-line items, but it wasn't until recently that the company made a decision to upgrade its packaging on a par with its contents. Now labels and packages have been redesigned for a more elegant look, and Sarotti is going head-to-head with such august competitors as Tobler and Lindt.

Sarotti chocolates are quite reasonably priced (a 3.5–ounce bar goes for just a little over a dollar). They are now being distributed around North America in department store chains (Neiman Marcus, for one), delicatessens, and even in certain supermarkets. Write or call Hubbs Importing Corporation (U.S.) or I.D. Foods (Canada) for more detailed information.

SPRENGEL

THE CHOCOLATE IN SPRENGEL BARS IS TASTY, CREAMY, AND SMOOTH, AS BEFITS A product that has undergone three days of conching. The *"Alpenvollmilch,"* or milk chocolate, bar is meltingly mild, while the bittersweet *"Zartbitter"* is dark and zesty. Sprengel's marzipan is just grainy enough to stand up to its dark chocolate covering, resulting in a truly satisfying combination.

Unfortunately, the six best-selling Sprengel bars contain alcoholic-flavored cream fillings, and thus are unavailable in the United States. Canadian consumers will have to consult their provincial Liquor Commissioners concerning availability. But the rest of the Sprengel collection, including bar chocolate and bonbons, may be found at New York's Bremen House and Macy's Cellar, and at specialty food shops around North America. Contact C. & J. Willenborg, Inc. for more information on where these sweets are available.

ISRAEL

ELITE CHOCOLATES

ELITE CHOCOLATES LIVE UP TO THEIR PROMISE-FILLED NAME—AND THEY ARE kosher, besides. Elite's bittersweet or *"Chocolate Amer"* bar is rich and dark, with a strong chocolate flavor. This is a high-quality, dark chocolate lover's bar, that more than stands up to the more well-known competition. Elite also makes creditable hazelnut and almond bars, as well as a lovely plain milk chocolate bar.

Elite is not limited to bar chocolate: several tasty assortments are available, as is excellent cocoa. For those who love halva, the nutty sesame confection, Elite makes a wonderful chocolate-coated version.

Elite chocolates are widely available in supermarkets and gourmet food shops. Or contact Israeli Assorted Confections (I.A.C.) for the location nearest you in the United States; in Canada, contact Barenholtz Foods.

ITALY

GENSACO MARKETING, INC.

GENSACO, KNOWN IN NORTH AMERICA AS AN IMPORTER OF ITALIAN ESPRESSO machines, is also a purveyor of some delectable Italian chocolate by the piece. The dark chocolate filled with mousse-textured chocolate rum paste is heady and luscious—and packs a bit of a wallop. Sad to report, this chocolate contains a bit too much rum to be sold in the United States. Gensaco may soon take advantage of Canada's more liberal policy on this point, and offer these morsels north of the border. Another idea they've had is to try reformulating the chocolate with a lowered alcohol content that still allows it to retain its heavenly taste and texture.

Keep watching for Gensaco's new formulation and meanwhile, enjoy nibbling on the Italian original when in Rome.

MOTTA CHOCOLATES

WHAT'S MORE DELECTABLE THAN A PLATE OF STEAMING PASTA? IF YOU'RE A CHOCO-late gourmet, the answer is delightfully clear: a plate of Motta chocolate ravioli. This improvement on the original version has a shiny dark chocolate exterior and a heavenly hazelnut praline filling. And for those chocolate lovers with a piscatorial preference? You guessed it—a verita-ble aquarium of chocolate seafood. Motta makes rich dark chocolate oysters with a luxurious champagne praline filling, dark chocolate cockle shells filled with almond and hazelnut praline, and milk chocolate escargots with hazelnut praline centers.

The Italian love of ice cream is celebrated with Motta's tribute to the ice cream cone, a semisweet chocolate *"Conetto,"* filled with cocoa cream and topped with crunchy hazelnut praline. Again, it's an improvement on the everyday item it so cleverly copies.

The Motta line is already well-known in Italy, and is now widely distributed in the United States and Canada at gourmet and specialty food shops, as well as at Eaton's department stores.

PERNIGOTTI

PERNIGOTTI HAS BEEN IN THE CHOCOLATE BUSINESS SINCE 1860, MAKING IT THE dean of Italian chocolatiers, with the experience and confidence that goes with the title. Ingredients such as South American and African cocoa, Italian and Spanish almonds, and honey from a small Mexican village in the Yucatan are used to create chocolates that have a heavenly strong chocolate perfume—and a taste to match.

Individually foil-wrapped, chocolate-covered walnuts and chestnuts are splendidly nutty, the chocolate hazelnut *gianduiotti* a creamy yet crunchy marvel. Pernigotti also makes superlative *torrone*, the chewy Italian nougat and nut delight that benefits greatly from a dark chocolate coating. Pernigotti's mouthwateringly smooth, not too sweet, dark chocolate *gianduia* bar gets its unique flavor from Piedmont hazelnuts.

On the West Coast, sample Pernigotti's *gelato:* the superb Italian ice cream that is lovely in every flavor, but best of all, naturally, in chocolate.

Pernigotti products are now available in the United States, with an emphasis on the West Coast, and throughout Canada. Check Fabio Imports for the location nearest you.

PERUGINA CHOCOLATES & CONFECTIONS, INC.

MENTION ITALIAN CHOCOLATES AND MOST PEOPLE IMMEDIATELY SAY, "PERUGINA." Mention Perugina and most people promptly answer *"Baci." Baci,* which means "kisses" in Italian, are marvelous mouthfuls of whole and chopped hazelnuts from the town of Perugia (whence Perugina gets its name), surrounded by an ethereal chocolate mousse and covered in chocolate. Another Perugina treat is the superbly sophisticated hazelnut *gianduja,* a cocoa-dusted cylinder filled with the smoothest and lightest of hazelnut cream. For those who like their hazelnuts whole, the *"Tre Re"* gives us three perfect specimens, blanketed in dark chocolate bliss. Perugina also makes a luscious dark chocolate buttercream.

Such delectable originals deserve special treatment, and Perugina's chic, stylish packaging is more than up to the task. The boxes are pretty enough to treasure long after the chocolate they once contained has been happily plundered. Some of the standouts are the "Imperial Egg," an inspired recreation of a precious jeweled Fabergé egg, and a "Christmas Card Box" with a woven straw cover depicting a folkloric Italian wine label.

Like many fine chocolate companies, Perugina is a family operation. But in this case, the family is the Buitoni's—purveyors of pasta the world over. Pepino Buitoni started the company in 1907, and members of the Buitoni clan have been making Perugina's confections ever since.

In New York City, Perugina chocolates are snugly ensconced in their own little jewel of a shop. Around the United States, Perugina is available at many of the better department stores, while Canadians may find it in Eaton's, Simpson's, and neighborhood Italian specialty shops. The Canadian distributor is Excelsior Brands, Ltd.; in the United States, Perugina is its own importer.

JAPAN

AKUTAGAWA CONFECTIONERY CO., LTD.

LEAVE IT TO JAPANESE TECHNOLOGY TO INVENT SOLID MILK CHOCOLATE MICROCOMputers, calculators, cameras, cassette radios, and electric razors! These items taste rather ordinary, but their whimsically detailed shapes are anything but.

Worthy of a chocolate lover's more serious attention is Akutagawa's elegant "Piaffer" line, which features beautifully packaged thin wafers of milk, dark, and white chocolate, each sporting a contrasting chocolate finely-wrought, raised horsehead design in its center. These chocolates are smoothly creamy, and their good breeding is evident in every bite. For those who love horses, or those who appreciate attractive chocolates, Piaffer would be a thoroughbred choice.

Akutagawa novelty and Piaffer chocolates enjoy wide distribution in the United States in gourmet and specialty shops, as well as in Canadian stores such as Eaton's. Contact Toha Trading, Inc. for the United States and Morris National for Canadian distribution information.

NETHERLANDS

A. DRIESSEN CHOCOLADEFABRIK

DISTINCTIVELY PACKAGED ALONGSIDE DELFT BLUE TILES DEPICTING CHARMING windmill scenes, Driessen chocolates are quintessentially, delightfully Dutch. Their smooth dark chocolate is high in cocoa butter content and tastes accordingly rich. Driessen milk chocolate is mellow, soft, and sure to please the North American palate. Each chocolate is embossed with the lion emblem that is the Netherlands' national insignia.

If you've flown on KLM Airlines, chances are you've already enjoyed Driessen chocolates, as they are the Dutch airline's official supplier. But even if you're not Amsterdam bound, you will soon be able to enjoy Driessen's chocolate medallions, cat's tongues, and filled chocolates with hazelnuts, orange, caramel, and mocha, just to name a few, at gourmet and gift shops across the United States.

DROSTE

THE NAME DROSTE IS PRACTICALLY SYNONYMOUS WITH DUTCH CHOCOLATE, AND IS A a perfect exemplar of the genre. Droste chocolates have a rich, smooth, creamy texture much loved by American chocolate connoisseurs of all ages.

Droste pastilles—solid milk, dark, or combination milk and dark round wafers—seem to dissolve on the tongue, but you may prefer to chew them and experience their satisfying chocolate solidity.

Droste also makes solid thin chocolate pieces with charming Dutch motifs: a white chocolate tulip on a milk chocolate background, and light and dark chocolate ears of corn, symbolizing Holland's agricultural heritage.

Filled chocolates are also made by Droste, and showcased in the "Royal Assortment." This eye-catching bright blue box, filled with tasty pralines in such flavors as hazelnut, cream caramel, chocolate caramel, maraschino cherry, and brandy, should take people's perception of Droste chocolate far beyond the pastille.

Cocoa is still a major part of Droste's line, and its legendary smoothness and solubility make it a natural choice for both drinking and baking.

All Droste products are widely available in stores throughout North America.

VAN HOUTEN

IT WAS COENRAAD JOHANNES VAN HOUTEN WHO IN 1828 DEVELOPED THE PROCESS known as "Dutching," making cocoa powder more digestible, yet intensely chocolatey. Today Van Houten is still known for its cocoa powder and cocoa butter, as well as for its eating chocolates.

Among the most popular are the "Choco Air," a bar that consists of aerated milk chocolate and tastes lusciously light and pleasing. (Its unique texture is akin to biting into a chocolate honeycomb, making the bar tremendous fun to eat.) The "Chocoladies" bar, available in dark or milk chocolate, isn't really a bar at all, but eighteen bite-sized morsels of excellent solid chocolate.

Van Houten assortments feature truffles and other filled chocolates, proving once again that the Dutch know what to do with chocolate.

Van Houten Chocolates are available throughout North America at gourmet and specialty shops. You may also want to check with the importers, Aristo International in the United States and Comet in Canada.

PORTUGAL

REGINA CHOCOLATES

REGINA, A PORTUGUESE CHOCOLATE FIRM THAT HAS BEEN IN BUSINESS SINCE THE early 1900s, makes chocolates in amusing novelty shapes such as umbrellas, pencils, and hearts. However, it is their smooth texture that should please the serious chocolate eater. These chocolates are not overly sweet and have no cloying aftertaste. Regina also makes the "Deauville," a fine bar of baking chocolate.

Regina chocolates are available in Portuguese ethnic stores in San Jose, CA, and New Bedford, MA, or contact the importer, Cortco International Corp., for more information.

SCOTLAND

J. & A. FERGUSON LTD.

FOR WELL OVER A CENTURY, J. & A. FERGUSON HAS BEEN MAKING ITS EXCELLENT ebony-colored chocolates (never milk), using cocoa beans from South America and the purest natural ingredients. These marvelously "bonny" chocolates for true aficionados are hand dipped and appealingly unassuming in appearance. The art is in their flavors: the richness of a truffle combining fresh cream, Scotch whisky, and that luscious dark, dark chocolate—or that same chocolate coupled with an exquisite icy mint or spicy ginger.

The dignified "Nine Reigns" box assortment celebrates the nine British monarchs, from King George III to Queen Elizabeth II, who have reigned during the company's existence. Offering truffles, pralines, nuts, and creams, this assortment of Ferguson's best is surely fit for a King or Queen—as well as for the rest of us commoners.

Ferguson is already exporting its wares to chocolate lovers in the Mideast and Japan, and plans to offer its specialties to the United States and Canada in the near future. Check gourmet stores and specialty shops before the queue forms, or write to the manufacturer directly for information. If you've tasted these sweets abroad, you'll know they're well worth waiting for.

SWEDEN

NORDCHOKLAD

SWEDISH NORDCHOKLAD EXPORTS BITTERSWEET AND MILK, FILLED AND SOLID chocolates. All are tasty and smooth. The simple milk varieties are especially pleasant and creamy. Even without any alcohol content, Nordchoklad's cordials are fruity chocolate pick-me-ups. The "Present" assortment is Nordchoklad's most lavish. Beneath its pretty package are a variety of fine chocolate bonbons.

You can find Nordchoklad in gourmet and specialty stores, or contact Atalanta Corporation for more information.

CLOETTA

SWEDISH CLOETTA CHOCOLATE IS DELIGHTFULLY MILD, AND IT COMES IN A VARIETY of "designer" bars, amusingly packaged in a denim, blue jean–decorated wrapper. Flavors include milk; mild bitter; and "nut milk," with roasted whole and chopped hazelnuts generously scattered throughout. Cloetta's "Orange Slices," shaped like the real thing, combine creamy milk chocolate or sophisticated bittersweet chocolate with the essence of oranges, to produce a lovely dessert accompaniment to a cup of strong coffee.

Cloetta chocolates are available in gourmet and specialty shops in the United States. Although these sweets are not yet distributed in Canada, Americans can check with André Proust, the importer, for a location near them. The distribution situation is in constant flux, so it can't hurt to write for information about possible future Canadian availability.

SWITZERLAND

CAILLER

CAILLER, WHICH BILLS ITSELF AS "THE PREFERRED CHOCOLATE OF SWITZERLAND," is certain to gain preference with anyone who likes luscious, rich, flavorful bar chocolate.

Their flagship bar is the *"Frigor,"* delectable thick milk chocolate filled with a creamy ganache center accented with ground almonds and hazelnuts. The *"Crémant,"* a deep, dark, and thoroughly delicious bar, can be used for cooking, although you'll probably want to buy extras to eat on their own. Also exemplary is Cailler's "Creamy White with Honey" bar, which is aerated to give it a lighter-than-air consistency.

Cailler bars are available in department stores and gourmet shops, or contact their importer, Jaret International.

HONOLD
Confiserie Suisse

ANYONE WHO HAS SAMPLED THE EXQUISITE CONFECTIONS OF ZURICH'S CONFISERIE Honold will be delighted to learn that this famed outpost of chocolate excellence now has a North American outlet. The Philadelphia shop carries all of Honold's chocolates, with the exception of the liqueur-filled chocolate strawberries and other items with too high an alcohol content for our austere American legal limits. Luckily, they do have Honold's truffles, whose heavenly liqueur flavoring and buttery ganache fillings add up to bittersweet ethereal chocolate ecstasy. These are small, dainty truffles that resemble pretty little jewels—with an appropriately precious chocolate taste and aroma. Standouts among Honold's truffles are the sprightly champagne, with a flavor so irresistible that it is nearly impossible to stop at one; and the sunny-flavored Grand Marnier, whose orange taste will instantly perk up your mouth.

Honold's chocolate-covered chocolate caramels are rich and silken, meltingly digestible. The mocha *gianduja,* too, is special, with its expert blending of crunchy hazelnut and aromatic coffee, with the unifying theme of superb Swiss chocolate tying it all expertly together.

Visit the Philadelphia shop, or contact them for mail-order information; they will ship to destinations throughout the United States and Canada. Honold's truffles are now also available at Saks Fifth Avenue.

HUTTMACHER CHOCOLATES
Confiserie Bosshard

IF YOU GET A KICK FROM CHAMPAGNE, YOU'LL GET A THRILL OUT OF CONFISERIE Suisse's *"Champagne Truffes,"* imported by Huttmacher from Switzerland's justly renowned Confiserie Bosshard of Winterthur. This splendid truffle has a milk chocolate exterior dusted with white powdered sugar, and is filled with an irresistible combination of light, creamy chocolate and champagne. Other truffles in such tempting flavors as cognac, kirsch, and rum succeed in marrying the exquisite essence of alcohol with the smoothness of chocolate—a match made in chocolate-lovers' heaven. Nonalcoholic flavors such as mocha, vanilla, milk, and *gianduia* are equally pleasing.

Huttmacher Enterprises, which distributes the chocolates, is strictly a mail-order operation. They will ship Bosshard's truffles and "Fleurette Blossoms" (solid delectable Swiss chocolate in flat round disks embossed with pretty floral designs) by UPS. Chocolates are not shipped, however, from June on until the hot weather has safely ended.

Of course, if you're in Switzerland, a visit to the Confiserie Bosshard of Winterthur is definitely in order. There you may sample its chocolates as well as its delightful pastries in the spot where they are made.

LINDT CHOCOLATES

ASK A CHOCOLATE MAVEN THE NAME OF HIS OR HER FAVORITE SWISS CHOCOLATES and the answer is likely to be Lindt. The venerable firm of Lindt and Sprüngli has been making its ultrasmooth, melt-on-the-tongue chocolate since the turn of the century, and in many ways, Lindt exemplifies the best chocolate there is—certainly the best being mass-produced.

The story behind the success is actually a crucial chapter in the history of chocolate. It starts with David Sprüngli, who apprenticed with a pastry shop and eventually became its owner. In 1845, Sprüngli's sons used the operation to found a popular chocolate factory. In 1899 the astute Sprüngli family purchased Rodolphe Lindt's chocolate operation in Berne, including his secret method of conching, for 1.5 million gold francs. Nowadays, the fifth and sixth generations of Sprünglis are producing magical chocolates under the Lindt name.

Under the Sprungli's, chocolate making has become an exact science. The "Lindt and Sprungli Chocolate Process" (which they abbreviate as LSCP) removes undesirable properties from the chocolate before it is refined. Milling is controlled to produce smaller-sized chocolate particles, allowing for more chocolate flavor in each drop. Temperature and pressure are regulated, producing an attractive silky sheen on the chocolate that minimizes "blooming" (discoloration of chocolate).

As with all fine chocolatiers, at Lindt, quality of ingredients is key. The cocoa beans used are South American. Each bean is first examined and graded for appearance and aroma. Then the famous Swiss technology enters the picture. Beans are roasted and undergo chromatography to determine whether they have been exposed to pesticides. Lindt's sugar is also tested for lumpiness, purity, and melting properties. A "rancidity meter," in which almonds, pistachios, and hazelnuts are exposed to an electric current, is used to reveal the nuts' freshness.

Production of Lindt's chocolate stresses cleanliness and efficiency, and makes full use of automation and technology. Quality checks take place at each stage of production, and Rodolphe Lindt's original conch is still used at regular intervals as a means for comparing the quality of the chocolate made then with today's product.

Indeed, "today's product" nobly carries on Lindt's tradition of chocolate excellence. It is admirably smooth and creamy, meltingly delicious, and has no bitter aftertaste. Nowhere are these attributes more apparent than in the Lindt *"Surfin"* bar—the deceptively simple dark chocolate masterpiece still being made from Lindt's original recipe. This chocolate has snap and substance. It is so far from being overly sweet that it might not be everyone's choice, but it is a true chocolate lover's bar, whose splendid unadulterated essence virtually bursts onto the tongue. The *Surfin* bar is also ideal for cooking (especially in the large thirteen-ounce "family size").

Lindt's plethora of high-quality bars includes flavors to please every palate. Especially tasty are the plain Swiss milk chocolate, the *"Alba,"* a milk chocolate bar with whole almond and marzipan filling, the raspberry-filled milk chocolate bar, and the *"Chocoletti,"* eighteen dark chocolate pieces with truffle filling, assembled in bar shape. Also delicious are Lindt's "Thins"—bittersweet or milk chocolate wafer-thin squares, perfect for savoring as they melt in the mouth.

Lindt also makes estimable boxed chocolates: shiny, appetizing morsels with delicious assorted fillings. Among the best pieces are the *"Carmenna,"* milk and dark chocolate surrounding a smooth butterscotchy caramel; the *"Truffina,"* dark chocolate over a bittersweet truffle center; the *"Rocher,"* with a soft milk chocolate outside and a delightfully crunchy almond praline center; and the *"Pineapple Cream,"* whose pleasantly tart center is an appealing foil to its bittersweet chocolate jacket.

Lindt chocolates are widely available in the United States as well as Canada. They can be found in department and retail stores, and even in the gourmet sections of certain supermarkets.

MOREAU CHOCOLATS INC.

SWISS MOREAU CHOCOLATES ARE KNOWN FOR THEIR DISTINCT CREAMY SMOOTH texture and their superlative ingredients: superior Venezuelan and Central American cocoa beans, cocoa butter, and a reduced amount of sugar (each crystal is specially refined to insure that its consistency is never gritty). Fresh cream from Switzerland's Jura Mountains, hazelnuts from Italy, and almonds from California are used. The Moreau factory was founded in 1882. It is still family owned and operated, and the chocolate recipes have not been altered in seventy-five years—a fine example of the quality of tradition.

Indeed, after tasting these delicacies, one realizes that there is no need to tamper with excellence. And eaters of Moreau chocolates are in good company: Rolls Royce, Cartier, Piaget, Rolex, and Mercedes Benz are longtime Moreau customers, for whom the company creates exquisite chocolates shaped like tiny cars, watches, etc., to be given as corporate gifts. The rest of us, however, can savor such delicious pieces as the *"Framboise,"* a silky smooth milk chocolate filled with raspberry purée; the *"Figaro,"* a combination of milk chocolate and chopped almonds, the dark chocolate nougat; and the zesty orange marzipan; as well as beautifully molded chocolate Swiss soldiers, lions, and horses, which are as lovely to look at as they are to eat.

You know you're staying at a great hotel when you find a Moreau chocolate on your pillow at night. These sweet dreams are available at the Biltmore in Phoenix, AZ. You can purchase Moreau chocolates in New York at Balducci's, DDL Foodshow, and Bloomingdale's; in Chicago at Marshall Fields and Treasure Island; in Austin, TX, at Higginbottoms and Sakowitz; in Pittsburgh, PA, at Creative Chocolates; in San Francisco at Confetti and I. Magnin; in Sacramento at Kaylah Chocolatier; in Boston at Sweet Temptations; in Anchorage at Nordstrom's; and in Seattle at Au Chocolat. Canadian chocolate lovers can request mail order delivery at many of these stores, or contact Moreau for additional information.

NEUCHÂTEL CHOCOLATES

NEUCHÂTEL CHOCOLATES ARE HOUSED IN A PRETTY PINK CONFECTION OF A SHOP, replete with pink branches on the ceiling and mirrors on all sides. This sweet setting is ideal for dainty, delicate chocolates, and Neuchâtel's do not disappoint.

Neuchâtel has a unique approach to candymaking. The chocolate itself is flown in weekly in bulk from Switzerland. Then it is transported to the Neuchâtel factory on Long Island, where chef Albert Lauber (himself a Swiss import and fifth-generation chocolate maker) creates Swiss chocolate delicacies that maintain the integrity of their motherland and the freshness without which no chocolate, imported or domestic, is worth eating.

In true Swiss tradition, Neuchâtel's truffles are splendid. Among the standouts are an unexpectedly alluring banana: buttery, smooth, and subtle, and blanketed with a white chocolate shell; the Grand Marnier, a spirited blend of orange liqueur and chocolate; and the hazelnut, whose light and airy filling has a distinctive nutty taste and a charming contrasting crunch. Neuchâtel also offers three different kinds of marzipan, and a generous assortment of buttercreams, pralines, and fruits.

"We've been experimenting to make excellent European chocolate that would also please the American public," explains proprietor Krikor Yepremian. Judging from the chocolates, the experiment is a rousing success.

Neuchâtel chocolates are available in four New York locations, as well as in Los Angeles, New Mexico, Chicago, Boston, and New Jersey, among others. They will also ship chocolates all over North America, but only from Labor Day to Memorial Day.

TEUSCHER

IF COLE PORTER HAD TASTED THIS SHOP'S INCREDIBLE CREATIONS, HE MIGHT HAVE written:

You're the top, you're De la Renta's ruffles.
You're the top, you're Teuscher's truffles.

Teuscher has been creating traditional hand-dipped chocolates in Zurich for over fifty years. Today, these superb Swiss chocolates are flown into the United States and Canada at the rate of at least once, often twice, a week, where they are snatched up by the cognoscenti almost as quickly as they arrive.

For truffle aficionados, Teuscher's champagne variety will become the toast of any town. These extra smooth, melt-in-the-mouth morsels, with the delectable sparkle of a champagne cream center, are a true celebration of chocolate-making. Equally splendid truffles are the praline, with its light gentle crunch and delicate whipped interior; the dark chocolate, which is sophisticated, buttery, and not too sweet; and the far-from-humble milk chocolate, which, by its exemplary blending of characteristically creamy Swiss chocolate flavor, proves that sometimes the simplest is best of all. These truffles more than merit their reputation as the standard against which all other competitors ultimately must be judged and found wanting.

Lest you get the mistaken idea that Teuscher's only makes thoroughbred truffles, be sure to try some of their other offerings: hazelnut and honey praline, marzipan, nougats, and fruit and solid chocolate centers. All are made without additives or preservatives, and each maintains that essential Swiss purity and smoothness.

Another delightful aspect of Teuscher is its imaginative decor and packaging. The brainchild of Zurich designer Felix Daetwyler, the cheerful sprightly decorations of animals, butterflies, and adorable insects, fashioned in brightly colored paper, give Teuscher chocolates a properly festive, lighthearted backdrop. Among the intoxicating blend of riotous colors and delightful cocoa aroma, every visitor, regardless of age or stature, is magically transformed into the proverbial "kid in the candy shop."

Teuscher chocolates are available at two New York locations, as well as at shops in Houston, Beverly Hills, and Toronto. Teuscher will also mail order its chocolates to sweet-lovers all over the United States and Canada.

TOBLER-SUCHARD U.S.A.

SWISS CHOCOLATE FANS REJOICE! TOBLER AND SUCHARD, TWO OF SWITZERLAND'S oldest and finest chocolate producers, have joined financial forces, while still producing their unique formulations independently of one another. However, their availability to North Americans will be enhanced.

Both these companies share certain characteristics: their chocolates are smooth and creamy, and tend to melt most satisfyingly on the tongue. But each, of course, has its own specialties.

Tobler's claim to fame is unquestionably the *"Toblerone"* bar. It is triangular, to resemble the Swiss Alps. And indeed, its luscious blending of milk chocolate, almond, and honey nougat has a special alpine freshness. A tired mountaineer who knew that a bite of *Toblerone* was waiting at the summit would surely muster the strength to go on. *Toblerone* are also inspirational in bittersweet and white chocolate formulations—both of which are delicious, yet perhaps a bit less distinguished than the traditional milk chocolate version.

Suchard is best known for its *"Milka"* bar, a classic chunk of pure, unadulterated milk chocolate, redolent of sweet meadow freshness, and its *"Bittra,"* a bittersweet bar chock-full of smooth, dark good taste, equally suited to both cooking and munching.

Both companies make a wide assortment of chocolate bars to suit every taste. Among the best are Tobler's *"Extra Bitter"* and *"Tradition,"* favored by chefs; and Suchard's *"Almond Milka,"* in which the nuts add a certain substance to their ultrasmooth chocolate surroundings. Both companies also produce high-quality boxed assortments in the inimitable Swiss tradition.

Tobler and Suchard chocolates are widely available in department stores and gourmet food shops throughout North America. Tobler U.S.A. is the American distributor, David Ashley, the Canadian name to contact.

UNITED KINGDOM

BENDICKS OF MAYFAIR

BENDICKS, MAKERS OF THE RENOWNED "BITTERMINTS", TONGUE-TINGLING MORSELS of peppermint fondant coated in rapturously bittersweet chocolate, are also the purveyors of excellent nonminted chocolates. All use top-quality raw materials, such as special Trinidad cocoa beans, and most are hand finished. This concern with quality has paid off, for Bendicks has been awarded the Royal Warrant.

Among their specialties are zesty chocolate ginger, nutty chocolate brazils, and the ever-popular chocolate truffles. Bendicks also produces superb "Sporting and Military Chocolate," a rich, bittersweet bar to be savored by all whose passion is true dark chocolate.

Bendicks chocolates are available in their seven London shops, as well as in Harrod's and Fortnum and Mason. In the United States, Bendicks chocolates can be found in Macy's and Bloomingdale's. In Canada, they are available at Woodward's and Eaton's. Hamstra and Walter Jacques are the American and Canadian importers, respectively.

CADBURY LIMITED

CADBURY'S DAIRY MILK CHOCOLATE IS CELEBRATED BY CHOCOLATE BAR CONNOIS-
seurs worldwide for its distinctive mellow taste and smooth, creamy
texture. When used by Cadbury, the words "dairy milk" mean that
Cadbury's milk chocolate is made with fresh, full cream liquid milk, not
the usual skimmed, dried milk favored by many other chocolate makers.
Cadbury's milk, collected daily from farms in areas that are known for
their high-quality dairy products, has a rich, full-bodied taste. In
contrast, the milk chocolate that is based on skimmed, dried milk sadly
lacks that real milk flavor.

Cadbury milk chocolate is at its best in a thick, plain classic bar. It is
also appealing, however, when paired with that irresistible high energy
combo of raisins and almonds, or with crunchy whole hazelnuts. These
bars will sustain the hardest-working hiker, as well as perk up the more
sedentary chocolate fanciers.

Purists will enjoy Cadbury's "Bournville" bar, a pleasing slab of smooth
dark semisweet chocolate. And those who crave something a bit different
in texture—but still emphatically chocolate—will find the answer in
Cadbury's "Flakes." This is a silly but descriptive name for log-shaped
pieces of textured milk chocolate. Flakes are eminently suitable for
eating as is, or for being broken up into fine, feathery chocolate splinters
and sprinkled decoratively and deliciously on ice cream, cakes, or
whatever else strikes your fancy.

Cadbury products are available throughout the United Kingdom and
North America.

CHARBONNEL ET WALKER

"PROBABLY THE BEST CHOCOLATES IN THE WORLD," IS THE MOTTO OF THIS EXCLU-
sive British firm, and there are many who agree—including the Queen,
who has granted them the Royal Warrant. These chocolates are dark and
delicious. They are still made according to the original recipes of
Mademoiselle Charbonnel, sometimes even using the original Victorian
molds.

Among the best are the daintily fragrant rose and violet creams
covered in rich dark chocolate, and the "Charbonnels," dark chocolate
sticks with a crispy mint interior. Charbonnel also makes excellent
chocolate ginger, caramels, pralines, and truffles.

As befits such genteel, high-quality bonbons, they are impeccably
packaged. Assortments may be purchased in *boites blanches*, Victorian-
style round white boxes with the firm's logo stamped in gold, fastened
with hand-tied thick satin bows. Inside, Charbonnel will prepare the
message of your choice, spelled out in molded chocolate letters covered
in gold foil—truly an impressive presentation. Other examples of Charbonnel's prestige packaging are the "Cigar Drum," packed with mocha
crisp batons wrapped in gold foil, and the "Theatre Box," an assortment
of bonbons prettily displayed in a round floral box tied with a pink satin
cord.

Charbonnel shops are located on London's Old Bond and Throgmorton Streets; the chocolates are also available in selected London hotels and confectioners. Those on the other side of the Atlantic—or anywhere else in the world—who wish to sample these top-notch delicacies need only request mail-order delivery, and Charbonnel et Walker will be happy to oblige.

ELIZABETH SHAW

ELIZABETH SHAW MAKES ONLY ONE CHOCOLATE, BUT AFTER A HEARTY DINNER you'll find that this clever mint is worth a queen's ransom. As it happens, Elizabeth Shaw's chocolate mint crisps are made by appointment to Elizabeth II, queen of England. If you are partial to smooth milk chocolate perked up with refreshing bits of crispy mint that you can see as well as taste, these should be a favorite of yours, too.

These savory delicacies are available throughout the United States in selected gourmet shops, or you may find them by contacting importer Christopher Reeves Brookes & Co.

FORTNUM & MASON

THIS VENERABLE GOURMET FOOD ESTABLISHMENT, WHICH HAS RECEIVED THE Royal Warrant, creates its own handmade traditional English chocolate delicacies. All are made according to the best old-fashioned recipes, using superb ingredients and top-notch techniques, as well as marble slabs and antique molds. Such British favorites as the sweetly perfumed rose and violet creams are exemplary here, as are the fresh and dainty strawberry and cream truffles and chocolate brandied cherries. In all, there are approximately fifty mouthwatering flavors from which to choose, plus a "Continental Range" of about thirty-five different shapes and flavors, not to mention a lovely assortment of Swiss truffles.

Fortnum & Mason's chocolates are only available at their Piccadilly, London shop. However, Fortnum & Mason will mail their splendid chocolates all over the world. Canadian connoisseurs can get these goodies through Eaton's department stores.

JOSEPH TERRY & SONS LIMITED
The Chocolate Works

IN OVER TWO HUNDRED YEARS OF PRODUCTION, JOSEPH TERRY HAS BUILT A SOLID and deserved reputation for superior chocolate. The firm is dedicated to high quality, and is extremely selective in choosing, blending, and roasting the cocoa beans that go into its dark, rich, bitter chocolate and smooth, creamy "Devon Milk" milk chocolate.

The highlight of Terry's offerings is its milk chocolate orange, a felicitous blend of milk chocolate to which genuine orange oil has been added. The result is a warm and sunny confection with a pleasant, though not overly sweet, orange taste that beautifully complements the solid milk chocolate. Shaped like a real orange divided into twenty individual segments, this chocolate is an impressive dessert.

Terry's is also noted for its "All Gold" dark chocolate assortment, a veritable treasure trove of delicious flavors. Inside the lid, a helpful legend guides you to the candy of your choice. The "Truffle Surprise" is particularly successful, with its rich and sensual soft rum and walnut flavored fondant filling. The assortment also contains a singular coffee cream, with just the right amount of coffee to provide a slight bite; a wonderfully chewy Brazil nut caramel; and a zesty ginger cake.

Terry's chocolates are widely available throughout the United Kingdom and are exported to Canada (through Walter Jacques), Australia, the Middle East, and Europe.

J. W. THORNTON LIMITED

THORNTON'S CHOCOLATES ARE LOCATED IN THE DALES OF YORKSHIRE AND DERBY-shire, the home of superb dairy ingredients. It is the rich, sweet cream dairy butter and milk that help give Thornton's chocolate its fresh and distinctive flavor.

Thornton's high quality is evident in such pieces as the milk chocolate "Rum Truffle," made with double cream and potent Jamaican rum—a tasty and intoxicating combination; the delicate "Lemon Parfait," in which deep dark chocolate acts as a perfect foil for a light, tangy lemon puree center; and the milk chocolate "Diplomat," which contains a crisp

and nutty chocolate almond praline filling. These pieces and more are available in Thornton's popular "Continental Assortment" (known as the "Oxford Assortment" in the United States)—an eye-catching collection that is a joy to sample.

Thornton's has over two hundred shops in the United Kingdom and four in the United States. The American shops are located in Chicago, Oakbrook, and Shaumburg, IL, and in Boston and Washington, D.C. Canadians can contact Walter Jacques for distribution information in the provinces.

MAYNARDS OF LONDON

MAYNARDS USES BELGIAN CALLEBAUT CHOCOLATE COUVERTURE TO MAKE THEIR pleasing dark and milk chocolates. Their chocolate ginger, in which pure Australian ginger is covered with a wash of chocolate, is soft, moist, and savory, with just enough bite to perk up even a jaded chocolate consumer. Maynards gives the same tasty treatment to chewy dates and marzipan. Try the milk chocolate–coated nougat bars for a satisfying snack.

Look for reasonably priced Maynards chocolates (the chocolate ginger goes for a mere $4–$5 a box) at gourmet or specialty shops, such as Laura Secord in Canada, or write directly to the manufacturer for information about where to find Maynards products near you.

UNITED STATES

ALETHEA'S

ALETHEA'S HAS BEEN MAKING OLD-WORLD-STYLE, HAND-DIPPED CHOCOLATES IN THE the Buffalo area for over forty years. As candymaker Dean Tassy points out, "We'd rather sacrifice quantity than quality." Production is limited and no preservatives are used: "this way we sell everything we make," Tassy says.

And no wonder. Alethea's makes its own savory marzipan, plus such unusual delicacies as tangy yogurt chocolate and exotic Chinese ginger fruit covered in dark chocolate. Alethea's dark chocolate is very dark, but without bitterness, and its smooth texture makes it a fine companion to any fruit. Also worth mention is Alethea's "chocolate covered sponge taffy" in which light and spongy molasses pillows get a lift from their chocolate drenching.

At the five Alethea shops in the Buffalo, NY, area, you can enjoy choosing whatever amount will sate you of creamy slab fudge, or—the ultimate for chocoholics—slab chocolate in dark, milk, and orange milk flavors. Try the orange milk, which has California cold-pressed orange oil blended right into it.

Prices here range from $5.95 to $9.95 per pound, depending on the assortment. Write or phone Alethea's for mail order information for the United States and Canada.

ANDRÉ BOLLIER LTD.
André's Confiseries Suisse

ANDRÉ'S IS THAT RARITY: A GENUINE, SOPHISTICATED SWISS *CONFISERIE*, IN THE heart of the American Midwest. Yet that unlikely location has no deleterious effect on the excellence and superiority of André's ultimate *truffes*, which Marcel Bollier, André's son, terms "the queen of chocolate candies." Savor the combination of soft-centered whipped cream and chocolate surrounded by a hard chocolate shell in such flavors as "*Truffe Madame*" (milk chocolate with chocolate ganache filling, covered with powdered sugar), "*Truffe Monsieur*" (vanilla bittersweet chocolate with chocolate ganache, dusted with cocoa powder), as well as bourbon, rum, Grand Marnier and white chocolate cognac *truffes*. The latter four flavors are sold only in the Kansas City, MO, store because of regulations prohibiting shipment of alcohol.

Also delicious are André's *rochers* (roasted, caramelized, slivered almonds covered with a thin coating of chocolate) and chocolate covered orange peel, the perfect accompaniment to a cup of coffee.

For a special gift, Marcel Bollier recommends André's unique wine bottle: an edible life-size bottle molded in milk or bittersweet vanilla chocolate and filled with 10 ounces of California raisins, then labeled with an original wine label.

André's has locations in St. Louis, Denver, Houston, and Menlo Park, CA. They will gladly fill mail or phone orders during the fall and winter, throughout the United States and Canada.

APHRODITE CONFECTIONS OF LOVE

FROM ONE SMALL RETAIL STORE THAT GOT ITS START ONLY THREE YEARS AGO, Aphrodite has become a burgeoning wholesale business. The Levine family, owners of Aphrodite, are justifiably proud of their chocolate confections, particularly what they term the "three T's": turtles, truffles, and toffee. Only pure ingredients are used, and their densely fudgy amaretto mousse will make mousse mavens' mouths water.

Aphrodite confections are available at such American locations as Bullock's, Bamberger's, Thalheimer's, Gimbel's, and John Wanamaker's, and across the Atlantic at Harrod's of Great Britain. Or you can sample their mousse at various Steak & Brew and Lindy's restaurants. They also send their confections throughout the United States and Canada, but it must be done through a wholesaler. Contact the store for more specific information about distribution.

ASTOR CHOCOLATE CORPORATION

IF YOU LIKE TO SIP YOUR AFTER-DINNER BRANDY OR LIQUEUR FROM A DEEP DARK chocolate cup, chances are that cup is made by Astor's. Coffee lovers can take Astor's milk chocolate mocha cup, fill it with whipped cream, and float it in a steaming cup of fresh brewed coffee. When the cup melts, it turns any coffee into an ambrosial brew.

Appropriately, Astor's other items are also associated with the finer things in life. The company makes chocolate dessert shells to fill at your whim, delicate after-dinner mints, and the pièce de résistance, a solid chocolate chess set of white and dark chocolate. It will set you back $70, but win or lose, the endgame will be sweet.

These products are made in Astor's New York factory, but they are available all around the United States in department stores and gourmet and specialty shops. Or write or phone Astor for information about locations nearest you. In Canada, the chocolates are distributed by Koster Imports of Montreal.

CATHERINE'S CHOCOLATES

FROM DEEP IN THE HEART OF NEW ENGLAND'S BEAUTIFUL BERKSHIRES COME excellent, homespun chocolates, celebrated both for their taste and their solid Yankee value.

Catherine Keretzes presides over this unpretentious little shop where, seven days a week, chocolates are lovingly hand dipped according to recipes that date back over a hundred years. Never one for following fads, Catherine continues to specialize in bittersweet chocolate "miniatures," which can be popped into the mouth all at once. Among her most successful offerings are splendid, buttery buttercrunch, the chocolate layer of which is enhanced rather than masked by its nutty coating; zesty "sponge chip" (molasses honeycombs dipped in dark chocolate), "peanut butter puffs," in which milk chocolate surrounds the creamiest, smoothest peanut butter; "nut delights" which blissfully blend milk or bittersweet chocolate, caramels, and pecans; and chocolate-covered cordial stem cherries that taste crisp, fresh, and strikingly adult rather than cloyingly sweet.

Catherine's now has a new location in Lenox, MA, closer to the Tanglewood crowd, but those of you who are far from New England need not despair. Catherine's will fill mail orders around the United States and Canada.

CHOCOLATE PHOTOS

EVEN THE MOST CAMERA SHY OF CHOCOLATE LOVERS IS APT TO BE SEDUCED INTO posing by the thought of his or her face embossed on squares of creamy milk or dark chocolate. Send your photo to Dr. Victor Syrmis, child psychiatrist and chocolate entrepreneur, and it will be used by artists to create a line drawing of your face. This image is then transferred to a magnesium mold and filled with freshly poured chocolate. And voilà! A recognizable one-inch square chocolate image, with your name underneath. Of course, along with your box full of chocolate pix and your photo reproduced on the inside wrapper, you get your original print back unharmed.

This lip-smacking exercise in self-promotion will set you back $35.00 a pound, $22.50 a half pound. The chocolate used is tasty, dependable Mercken's. Mail orders take two to four weeks to fill; for Canada, allow an extra week or so.

LE CHOCOLATIER

FAMED CHOCOLATIER HEINZ ROBERT GOLDSCHNEIDER, KNOWN MORE FAMILIARLY TO his legion of admirers as "Mr. Roberts," won deserved acclaim for his chocolate confections and disappointed many when he announced his retirement from candymaking. But Roberts' fans can now rejoice—Mr. Roberts' excellent European-style recipes are being made again, and under the name "Le Chocolatier" are available in two elegant outposts in Chicago and New York. (Plans for a future San Francisco store are in the offing.)

Le Chocolatier's white *truffe*, an ethereal blend of creamy milk chocolate splashed with Cointreau and topped with a dusting of confectioner's sugar, is both rich and light—truly exquisite. Also memorable are the "Java," a deep, dark chocolate and espresso combination, and the "Gianduja Marzipan," a sophisticated, layered delight that felicitously pairs the crunch of hazelnuts with the fine-grained texture of ground almonds, then binds the union with an unctuously dark chocolate coating.

Le Chocolatier's offerings are expensive ($25 per pound), but considering that each piece is hand-cut, hand-dipped, and lovely to look at, and that all come packaged in handsome burgundy and silver, the price of indulgence seems right. Le Chocolatier will ship by mail between October and April throughout the United States and Canada.

LE CHOCOLATIER

HOUSED IN A CHIC CONVERTED BARN, LE CHOCOLATIER OF LATHAM, NY, OFFERS AN eclectic assortment of chocolate delights ranging from chocolate-dipped fruits (such as seedless grapes, plump Australian apricots, figs, prunes, oranges, blueberries, and raspberries) and tasty hand-dipped chocolates made in the traditional manner, to superlative homemade ice cream in such lavishly rich flavors as chocolate buttercream. What makes ice cream cones truly special at Le Chocolatier is that the cones themselves are dipped in white chocolate before being filled with ice cream. Le Chocolatier also offers delicious boxed assortments from the venerable Lindt, Godiva, and Droste, and is experimenting with making its own chocolates on the premises.

While this chocolate barn is charming, Albanyites may choose to visit its parent branch of the same name on Hamilton Street. You can write or call in to place a mail order. Canadian orders will be shipped parcel post.

CIRCUIT CHIPS

KNOW ANY SILICON VALLEY CHOCOHOLICS? THEY, OR ANYONE ELSE WHO SPENDS A lot of time around computers, are bound to appreciate the good milk chocolate taste of "Circuit Chips:" seven-ounce replicas of computer chips, touted as "the chocolate computer buffs love to *byte*."

Circuit chips are packaged two boards to a box, and are a tasty high tech gift. Made of smooth, creamy chocolate, they may be the easiest thing to swallow about our present love affair with computers.

Interface with Byteware, Inc. in Lawrenceville, NJ, for information about where you can find Circuit Chips near you; you can place an old-fashioned mail or phone order for delivery anywhere in the United States or Canada.

CUMMINGS STUDIO CANDIES

OVER SIXTY FIVE YEARS AGO, V. CLYDE CUMMINGS SIGNED UP FOR A HIGH SCHOOL home economics class in order to be near a girl he liked. Cummings soon found that he liked the candymaking he learned in class almost as much as his sweetheart. In 1924 he opened a store, and developed the basic candy formulas still being used today by his son Paul.

"Dad was a genius at taste acuity," Paul says. After sampling Cummings' toothsome truffles, you'll know what he means. They are truffles with gusto: generously sized and smoothly satisfying on the tongue.

What makes hearty American-style Cummings chocolates so successful? A combination of South American Tehuantepec chocolate, very rich cream, Geneva milk, and most important, time. Extra time is needed to stir the chocolate after it has cooled (to achieve a finer grained, smoother product), and also for the hand-rolling and hand-dipping that are the hallmarks of superior chocolate production.

Other Cummings specialties are the three-flavor "Neapolitan Opera Bar," which is a tasty and attractive blend of cream, strawberry, and fudge; the soft, buttery caramel; and the refreshing double-dipped mints.

Cummings will fill mail orders around the United States. They will also mail to Canada from October 1 to May 1. With prices as reasonable as $6.95 per pound (plus an additional mailing charge), this is one of the best chocolate bargains around.

DILETTANTE CHOCOLATES

THE NAME MAY BE "DILETTANTE," BUT THESE WONDERFUL CHOCOLATES ARE IN NO way amateur. In fact, they are among the very best the United States has to offer—rich and possessed of an unequaled chocolate intensity.

Dilettante Chocolates are made from formulas created by Julius Franzen, a pastry chef who apprenticed in Budapest at the turn of the century. He served in St. Petersburg under Tsar Nicholas II, where he learned the secrets of chocolate making, which he later used as Master Candy Maker to Franz Josef I, the Austrian Emperor. At the time of World War I, Franzen emigrated to the United States, where he passed on his formulas to his brother-in-law, E. Remington Davenport. Today, Davenport's two grandsons are using those same formulas to delight discriminating and increasingly sophisticated North American palates.

Dilettante's "*Ephemere*" truffles (their best seller) are dark, dense, chocolate lovers' truffles, with a cocoa taste that is a revelation of clarity and truth. Equally splendid are the Grand Marnier and mocha truffles, rich in chocolate plus the added spice of orange liqueur or strong coffee essence. Those of you who prefer an excellent piece of "candy" (as opposed to the more serious truffles) will crave the *"Rheingold,"* a milk chocolate butter pecan toffee with spirit and crunch. This piece was commissioned by the Seattle Opera to commemorate their yearly performance of Wagner's Ring Cycle. Dilettante also makes tender, flaky marzipan, which has just the right amount of sweetness. In addition, you'll find rich buttercreams, among which the maple and bourbon varieties are standouts.

What to Do if Your "Local" Chocolatier Is Miles Away

Not everyone is lucky enough to live within sniffing distance of a favorite chocolatier, rejoicing each day in the aroma of newly made truffles. Indeed, many of us are not even within driving distance of true chocolate gratification. If you count yourself among those who live far away from the chocolate mainstream, you too can fulfill your chocolate dreams. Most major, high-quality department stores or gourmet food shops within catalog range will probably be glad to satiate your chocolate hunger by means of U.P.S. or mail delivery. Often, these stores are the sources of the best chocolate available.

All you need do is contact the store of your choice's confectionery department and ask if they fill mail order requests. Don't worry about your chocolates arriving in less than topnotch condition. Nowadays, improved packaging and more efficient delivery should enable you to receive your chocolate in perfect shape and in a very reasonable amount of time. (Some stores do not ship during the summer months, because they cannot ensure perfect delivery.) If for some reason the chocolates arrive in less than top form, immediately contact the store from which you ordered them; the store should replace the damaged goods tout de suite.

These chocolates are made in small, carefully controlled batches, with all natural flavorings. Dilettante chocolates have snap and taste. They are flavorful rather than merely sweet.

Such fine chocolates deserve special packaging, and Dilettante's elegant silver wrappings more than live up to the extraordinary candies they house. At $20 a pound, these chocolates are pricey, but genuine luxe is worth paying for.

There are presently three Dilettante stores in Seattle. At press time, plans were underway for another outlet in California. Aside from selling chocolates, the stores function as dessert restaurants, serving such chocolate delicacies as Dobos torte and other pastries, ice cream, and espresso. But if you can't visit a Dilettante store, don't despair—they will efficiently fill mail and phone orders in North America.

ETHEL M CHOCOLATES

THE ALL-AMERICAN CHOCOLATES IN THE OLD-FASHIONED-LOOKING, LACE-EMBOSSED beige box take their name from the mother of their creator, Forrest Mars. Perhaps you remember Mr. Mars from the candy bars of your childhood; these days he's putting his energy into tasty boxed chocolates, some with real liqueur fillings—for the grownup who's still got a bit of the kid inside. Unfortunately, the popular liqueur offerings such as "Cherries Jubilee" are only sold within the state of Nevada, where the law allows the combination of liqueurs with candy. But the next time you're in Las Vegas or Reno, remind yourself that these goodies are no gamble.

The rest of us can be more than content with Ethel M's nonalcoholic varieties: good, robust, dark chocolate creams and raspberry creams, caramels and nougats. In fact, Ethel M's nut offerings are especially good: the crunchy "Almond Butter Krisp," generously punctuated with almonds, and the irresistibly chewy milk chocolate "Pecan Patty."

Ethel M will fill mail orders for some chocolates. Please write or call toll-free for their brochure with more information. Or visit their shops in most of the major cities of Nevada and California. Unfortunately, they do not mail to Canada.

GABRIELLE'S FINE CHOCOLATES

MRS. GABRIELLE SEYFRIED MAKES SOPHISTICATED, BEAUTIFUL BELGIAN-STYLE chocolates—in New Jersey! She uses real fruit, heavy cream, and the best egg yolks and butter to create her lovely, delicate pieces. Gabrielle's chocolate contains no lecithin, only cocoa butter, which results in a smoother, softer, more fluid chocolate. Her cone-shaped dark chocolate coffee truffle has a marvelously subtle taste that gets better with each bite. Her raspberry cream has a delicate but definite fresh raspberry flavor—right down to the suggestion of a seed.

Gabrielle's chocolates are available in pleasing presentations, such as a chocolate clamshell filled with a half-pound assortment of filled chocolates, or a round chocolate box seven inches in diameter, filled with one and one-quarter pounds of assorted chocolates. Mail and phone orders are available in Canada and the United States from mid-September to the end of May, depending upon the weather.

GHIRARDELLI CHOCOLATE CO.

THOSE WHO HAVE VISITED SAN FRANCISCO'S FAMED GHIRARDELLI SQUARE HAVE probably tasted the fine American-style chocolate for which it was named. Ghirardelli chocolates, created by Italian Domingo Ghirardelli in 1849, have become an American tradition. Chocolate maker Ghirardelli is credited with patenting the process for making powdered chocolate. Today, his products include not only ground chocolate and cocoa, but semisweet chocolate chips and excellent unsweetened, semisweet, and sweet chocolate for baking and eating.

There is little in life to compare to the ecstasy of walking on Fisherman's Wharf and munching on Ghirardelli's "broken milk chocolate," thick, hearty slabs of chocolate perfect for sinking one's teeth into.

Other noteworthy Ghirardelli chocolates are the zesty "mint chocolate squares," and a variety of bars—including milk chocolate, milk chocolate with raisins, milk chocolate with almonds, and milk chocolate with crunchy malt.

Ghirardelli products are widely available in supermarkets and gourmet shops throughout the United States. Unfortunately, they are not yet available in Canada.

GODIVA CHOCOLATIER, INC.

IN THE MINDS (AND MOUTHS) OF MANY DEVOTED CHOCOLATE CONNOISSEURS, GODIVA and gourmet chocolates are synonymous. A name that formerly brought to mind images of a beautiful naked woman galloping on horseback has been displaced by that familiar gold ballotin tied in golden cord, an appropriately elegant container for the jewel-like chocolate bounty nestled within.

In recent years, Godiva's golden image has been slightly tarnished—when the populace learned that the maker of Belgian chocolates par excellence was being purchased by Campbell's Soup and would be operating out of Pennsylvania, many feared that the once proud chocolates would no longer be "Mmm—mmm—good." However, after tasting the chocolates, one is willing to forgive Godiva and forget that these pretty delicacies are no longer Belgian. What matters is that their taste and character stand up remarkably well.

Godiva concocts its chocolates from high-quality South American beans, and makes unstinting use of fresh heavy cream, dairy butter, and natural flavorings (artificial colors and preservatives are never used). Its shell-molding process is typically European in style: a chocolate shell is filled with the desired interior and topped with liquid chocolate. This method produces the exceptionally fine-looking seashells, starfish, tennis rackets, flowers, etc. that exemplify the Godiva look.

While many of the Godiva chocolates sold in the United States and Canada have the same formulation as in Belgium (without the alcohol, of course), others are new pieces, specially developed for the North American market. The challenge for Godiva has been to re-create their pieces without the alcohol, using liqueur flavorings instead of the genuine article. In general, this substitution has been accomplished quite skillfully. As for those pieces which could not be duplicated without kirsch, brandy, or rum, the company will not even attempt to remake them. Unfortunately, you'll have to travel to Belgium to experience the kirsch-flavored "vanilla crème walnut" or the "raisins with bourbon."

Chocolate Catering

How would you like chocolate placecards for your next party? Or a chocolate basket, filled to the brim with chocolate fruits and flowers, to be used as a centerpiece and eaten—by you—after your last guest has departed? No, this chocolate lover's dream is not too good to be true. Thanks to the chocolate caterers, now your parties and business functions can be catered in chocolate.

Foremost among this new breed of specialty caterers is California's Lee Gelfond, who uses her expertise to create gorgeous giant white chocolate swans, lifesize chocolate Christmas trees, intricate chocolate teacups and saucers, and other chocolate constructions that look—and are—good enough to eat. As you might expect, Gelfond's creations are costly. Molded chocolate placecards go for $2.50 apiece, and centerpieces start at $50.00, but what self-respecting, chocolate-loving bon vivant could resist?

Gelfond works with her own blends of Merckens, Guittard, and Callebaut chocolates, and claims she can copy any design you might request and faithfully render it in chocolate. She will be glad to send the results, as long as they are shippable. Contact her at: Chocolate by Lee Gelfond, 275 South Robertson Boulevard, Beverly Hills, CA 90211. Telephone (213) 854-3524.

But Americans and Canadians are far from deprived: Godiva still produces a range of delectable chocolates that need no alcohol to excite the palate. Among them are the praline almond with almond and filbert butter, the zesty cranberry cordial with actual pieces of cranberry rather than pulp—the berry's tartness provides a unique foil for the mellow chocolate—and the luscious milk chocolate piece filled with chocolate mousse. North Americans can also savor Godiva's crème fraîche pieces. Flown in from Belgium, they are the genuine, ambrosial article.

Godiva's latest innovation is none other than—you guessed it—the truffle. But these truffles are unlike any you have ever seen—or tasted—before. Those accustomed to the usual small, delicate pieces may well be shocked. These are enormous, the size of golf balls. They are also plump, rich morsels of chocolate goodness. The best may well be the vanilla truffle, whose gentle cream filling is laced with dark chocolate chips. Also distinctive are the chocolate truffle, with its mousselike interior, and its exterior of cocoa mixed with cinnamon; and the cherry truffle, with its smooth, dark, subtle filling, milk chocolate coating, and dusting of confectioner's sugar. While these truffles are all American-sized, there are plans afoot for a line of smaller truffles as well. These will have different flavors, but Godiva promises that they will maintain the same richness and chocolate base.

Lately Godiva has tried its hand at ice cream—a delicious, very high fat, extremely dense and flavorful chocolate treat—as well as delectable ice cream toppings. Their packaging, as always, is innovative and beautiful. And—lucky for us—Godiva products are widely available. They can be found in every major United States city, as well as in Canada, particularly in Montreal and Toronto. Canada not only carries American Godiva products, but also imports some pieces directly from Belgian Godiva.

HARBOR SWEETS

ANCHORS AWEIGH! THESE DELIGHTFUL PIECES WITH NAUTICAL MOTIFS ARE AMONG the very best chocolates America has to offer.

Ben Strohecker, a former marketing director at Schraffts Candy Co. and Keebler Biscuit Co., set out on his own ten years ago to try to produce "the best piece of candy in the world." And lo and behold, he's come awfully close. Strohecker uses ninety-three score Land O'Lakes butter, fresh cream, Mercken's Dark and Wilbur White chocolate to create his four signature pieces: the "Sweet Sloop," a sailboat-shaped piece of almond butter crunch covered with dark chocolate with a white chocolate mainsail and jib, and crushed pecan "spindrift" at the base; the "Sand Dollar," a soft, creamy, buttery caramel with pecans, covered in dark chocolate, and molded in a sand dollar shape; the "Marblehead Mint," bittersweet dark chocolate flecked with the crunch of peppermint, and embossed with a sailboat; and the "Barque Sarah," a piece of dark chocolate toasted almond bark, named for the ships that sailed from Salem, MA, to the Canary Islands in the 1850s.

Strohecker claims his candies are among the most expensive in the United States per pound, but the quality more than justifies the expense. The Sand Dollar, in particular, is a delightful piece of candy, a legitimate chunk of buried treasure. Besides, these uniquely American gourmet items still cost far less than their European competition.

Harbor Sweets' chocolates are available at gift shops around the United States, and, in slightly different incarnations, as promotional pieces for such institutions as New York City's Metropolitan Opera, the Boston Symphony Orchestra, the Museum of Fine Arts in Boston, and the Cleveland and Chicago symphony orchestras. Appropriately, Harbor was the 1984 official chocolatier to the Americas Cup yacht races.

Harbor Sweets' chocolates are also available through mail and phone orders, in Canada as well as the United States, and their hot weather packaging really does the trick. Each piece arrives individually wrapped in gold foil—fresh, moist, attractively presented, and sinfully delectable.

HARRY LONDON CANDIES, INC.

HARRY LONDON'S CHOCOLATE DELIGHTS TAKE NOVEL FORMS: A MILK CHOCOLATE bingo card that proclaims, "More than even chocolate (or bingo) itself... we love you!"; a milk chocolate football; a pair of chocolate "hot lips;" and a chocolate "get well pill" that should cure whatever ails you, especially if you suffer from periodic bouts of "chocolate withdrawal." These items are whimsical, funny, and taste good, too.

Harry London's also makes "London Mints," a tasty combination of peppermint and milk chocolate that has been enjoyed at the White House.

London's has forty stores in Ohio, and will take mail or phone order requests throughout North America for its four hundred items, which have brought chocolate good cheer to satisfied customers the world over.

JERBEAU HANDMADE CHOCOLATES

THESE THIRD GENERATION CHOCOLATE MAKERS REMAIN PURISTS—JERBEAU HAND-made Chocolates, as the name implies, are hand-rolled, hand-dipped, and hand-packed, and they contain neither preservatives nor waxes of any kind. What Jerbeau Chocolates do contain, however, is a plethora of excellent ingredients. Jerbeau's bittersweet chocolate is a blend of five different couvertures; their milk chocolate is a combination of American and Swiss couvertures. Jerbeau also uses real liquors, from which they extract their own flavoring essences.

All these fine ingredients are put to good use in Jerbeau's imaginative confections. The "Lehar," for instance, combines crushed burnt sugared almonds with bittersweet or milk chocolate for an extravagantly crunchy chocolate treat. The "Orange Nut" pairs bittersweet or milk chocolate with an almond marzipan coating containing crushed pecans, orange peel, and rum essence—the different tastes working together to provide a tangy, tongue-tingling blend.

Jerbeau's truffles are also noteworthy, particularly the "Mumm Champagne," with its sprightly center, and the "Classic Bittersweet," whose fudgy essence is sparked by a dash of Myers Rum flavoring.

Jerbeau Chocolates are available in New York City at Bloomingdale's, or can be ordered by mail to reach destinations anywhere in North America. Either way, you get the unique Jerbeau box, splotched with a child's chocolate handprint.

KARL BISSINGER FRENCH CONFECTIONS

IN THE NINETEENTH CENTURY, KARL FREDERICK BISSINGER WAS GIVEN THE TITLE OF "Confiseur Imperial" by French Emperor Louis Napoleon. Today the Bissinger tradition of fine chocolate making continues in the United States with Bissinger's famed "Chocolate Catalog." This compendium contains everything from edible chocolate dominoes to Stanley Marcus's (of department store Neiman Marcus fame) favorite piece: the pecan nut ball. Also inventoried is the best lollypop you'd ever want to bite into (and bite is the word)—rich, chewy caramel dipped in deep dark chocolate.

Bissinger's makes over three hundred kinds of superior chocolates. One highlight: fresh Oregon raspberries individually hand-covered with fondant, then dipped into milk or dark chocolate. These splendid berries are only available during the month of July, but you can receive them anywhere in North America by placing a mail or phone order.

Bissinger's is also known for its hand-decorated work, its custom-designed chocolate mints for parties, and the imaginaton and top-notch ingredients it uses in putting together its chocolate collection.

Write or call toll-free for mailing information.

Galerie Au Chocolat

These attractive and sophisticated shops house only the best imported French and Belgian hand-crafted, hand-molded chocolates. All are preservative and paraffin free, and contain thirty to forty percent less sugar—and correspondingly more flavor—than typical North American bonbons.

The concept behind the stores is a "chocolate gallery" that functions similarly to an art gallery, in which customers may enter and select each piece of chocolate as if it were an objet d'art or a piece of fine jewelry. And what a selection to choose from! There are 122 different pieces, each with its own special appeal. There is a striking "Champignon," or brown and white chocolate mushroom, with a deep dark chocolate–covered nougat cap and a white chocolate stem containing a lush and sensuous caramel interior. The "Perle d'Or," or golden pearl, is a gold foil-wrapped chocolate jewel, consisting of creamy ganache in a crisp nougat shell, surrounded by luscious milk chocolate. The unusual and captivating "Chardon Bleu," or blue thistle, consists of mellow toasted hazelnut praline, covered with smooth white chocolate that has been tinted pale blue with natural blueberry coloring. Also available are whimsical solid milk chocolate sardines and milk chocolate seashells with whipped chocolate centers.

So far, there are five Galerie Au Chocolat shops, in Cincinnati and Columbus, OH; Pittsburgh, PA; Annapolis, MD; and Norfolk, VA. Discriminating consumers will be pleased to know that more locations are planned. They take both phone and mail orders from throughout the United States and Canada.

KRON CHOCOLATIER, INC.

CHOCOLATIER PAR EXCELLENCE, TOM KRON LEARNED THE SECRETS OF HIS TRADE IN his native Hungary, and brought his own blend of European smoothness to his phenomenally successful big city chocolate boutiques.

Kron's chocolate possesses an abundance of cocoa butter, blended with high quality South American cocoa beans and just enough sugar so that the finished product melts in your hand—and in your mouth. His chocolate is ultra-refined, smooth, mellow, and luxurious, and is molded into cunningly irresistible objects: a woman's leg, a plump teddy bear, a tennis racket, even a chocolate telephone. When Kron fills his chocolates, he uses only "healthy" fillings, such as pleasantly tart juicy apricots, macadamia nuts, or Italian white cherries. Kron chocolate is made in his New York factory, but every Kron chocolatier dips its own luscious fruit daily. Try the orange slices in dark chocolate, and let your tongue rejoice at the bursts of fresh, sparkly, not-too-sweet goodness.

Kron shops are located around North America in such cities as Washington, DC, and Chicago.

If you find yourself in New York City, call (212) 982-4850 to arrange to take Kron's inimitable factory tour. For $25, you will taste and taste to your chocolate loving heart's content, while viewing the chocolate-making process from start to finish. Your tour guide is none other than Tom Kron himself—an original, just like his chocolates.

LILED'S CANDY KITCHEN

LILED'S IS A CANDY EMPORIUM CATERING TO LOYAL LOCALS IN THIS QUIET TOWN thirty miles north of San Francisco. Owner C. Henry Barner is a former management consultant who keeps a sharp eye on his delectable domain, hand dipping and making his chocolates himself, buying high quality ingredients (double whipping cream, sweet butter, and Guittard couverture) and making sure that each chocolate is polished to a shine with a special badger-hair brush prior to sale.

Favorites are Liled's satiny caramels ("They are nice and buttery, and won't interfere with dental work," Barner assures); "rocky road Easter eggs," in which the chocolate paste inside is combined with marshmallow and nuts; and the rich, velvety truffles, which are only made during holiday time because their shelf life is so short.

Liled's also makes its own ice cream, with such ambrosial flavors as "French Double Chocolate" and "Chocolate Showers" (like chocolate chip, but with fine-textured chocolate shavings), with chocolate amaretto and chocolate Grand Marnier leading the pack.

Prices are moderate: $6.50 for a one-pound assortment, $8.50 for a one-pound nut assortment. Liled's will mail chocolates throughout North America, but not during the summer months.

LISA LERNER CHOCOLATES

TRUFFLE FANATICS, TAKE HEART. "TRUFFLETIER" LISA LERNER HAS PROMISED NOT to deviate from her chosen profession: truffle making. Lerner mastered the art of confectionery in Switzerland, and she is one of the originators of that superb chocolate hybrid known as the "California truffle." Lerner's truffles are traditional in their allegiance to top-quality ingredients, such as pure chocolate, forty-two percent dairy fresh butterfat cream, freshly toasted nuts, fine liqueurs, and natural flavorings. However, they break new ground in several areas, namely their large size, hard chocolate–dipped shells, and innovative flavors.

Examples of Lerner's art are the "Dark Ultra Chocolate Truffle," whose velvety texture and supremely sophisticated bittersweet flavor make it a real chocolate lover's truffle; the "Dark Cognac Truffle," with mellow brandy and cream adding warmth to the smooth, voluptuous chocolate; and the "Cappucino Truffle," a delightful combo of milk chocolate and coffee, with just a hint of bite.

Lerner now makes her truffles in three sizes: the healthy California size, a medium size, and an adorable baby size. But whichever size you choose, your mouth is sure to be the winner.

Lisa Lerner Chocolates are available at specialty shops throughout the United States. Or you can write to her directly for mail order information for North America.

THE MAILLARD CORPORATION

THE MAILLARD CORPORATION MAKES ONE CHOCOLATE BAR, "MAILLARD EAGLE Sweet Chocolate," and a very special bar it is. Four ounces of high-grade, slightly-sweeter-than-bittersweet chocolate, the Eagle Sweet bar is favored by gourmets both for baking *and* eating. Expert chocolate chefs such as Maida Heatter specify its use in their recipes. Some people have been known to purchase a bar intending to bake with it—but when they open it up, sniff it, and take a nibble, they suddenly find they've eaten the entire bar! It's a good idea to buy more than one, so you can enjoy Eagle Sweet in both its incarnations.

Maillard Eagle Sweet Chocolate bars are available between New York and Chicago, but farther west and north distribution gets a bit spotty. If you contact the Maillard Corporation directly, they will tell you where their bars are sold.

MAVRAKOS CANDIES

MAVRAKOS CANDIES WAS FOUNDED BY GREEK IMMIGRANT JOHN MAVRAKOS IN 1907, and today consists of thirteen thriving shops in the St. Louis area. They produce over two hundred centers dipped in Nestlé chocolate coatings. Among the best are the "Pecan Burrs," a pleasing trio of pecan, caramel, and milk chocolate; "Heavenly Hash," a sweet blend of marshmallow, pecan, and milk chocolate; and the crunchy English toffee. Mavrakos also makes delectable chocolate covered strawberries.

A pound of Heavenly Hash costs $7.25, Pecan Burrs are $8.50, and assortments range from $5.95 to $6.95 per pound.

Call or write for mailing information. Mavrakos will take phone and mail orders and will send their chocolates anywhere in the world.

MILTON YORK FINE CANDIES

THE FIRST MILTON YORK CANDIES WERE SERVED IN 1882 IN A SMALL TOWN AT THE mouth of the Columbia River. Milton York's headquarters in those rugged days was a tent with the simple sign "Candy." His chocolates were cooked over an open fire fueled by native alderwood.

Today, Milton York candies are made in a modern factory, but their recipes are still the same, and they still contain pure whipping cream, Swiss chocolate, and natural flavors, and are without preservatives. Especially delicious are the milk chocolate "Velvets," which are halfway between a cream and a caramel in consistency; the "North Head Chocolate Mint," which takes its name from a local lighthouse; and the "Cranberry Jells," made with cranberries that grow in the nearby bogs, dipped into milk or dark chocolate. Another good bet is the "Milton York Special," a three-layered extravaganza of chopped almonds and dark chocolate, covered with milk chocolate.

There are three Milton York stores in the Long Beach, WA, area, and the company also fills mail and phone orders for the United States and Canada, except during the summer months. Prices are a bargain-range $6.50 to $7.50 per pound, plus an additional $2.85 for shipping.

MRS. LONDON'S BAKESHOP

FANS OF SARATOGA SPRINGS RETURN TO THIS DELIGHTFUL CITY FOR MANY REASONS: its splendid racetrack, its Victorian architecture, its cultural offerings, and its sparkling mineral water. But there is perhaps no more compelling inducement than Mrs. London's Bakeshop, a chocolate lover's dream come true. Nestled inside this bakery cum cafe, fitted with pink marble tables and old-fashioned floral sprigged wallpaper, are some of the most delectable chocolate treats imaginable.

Mrs. London's makes only two types of truffles, framboise and Grand Marnier, but they are both exceptional. These are truffles for traditionalists. Perfectly sized and prepared in accordance with the classical European method, these morsels of light and creamy chocolate are lovingly dusted with cocoa powder. Their flavoring contains just a hint of liqueur, enough to enhance the superb overall chocolate essence without overpowering. As is evident from their impeccable flavor, Mrs. London's truffles are fashioned from the best ingredients: Callebaut chocolate, sweet butter, and fresh, heavy cream. You may purchase them at the shop, either by the piece in a slim French truffle tube which holds nine truffles, or, when available, in an edible molded chocolate box filled to the brim with truffles.

Mrs. London's is probably best known for its splendid cakes and pastries. Their unique chocolate desserts are among the best you will find anywhere.

Mrs. London's Chocolaté Cake

This uniquely delicious chocolate cake is made without flour, which gives it a light, almost souffle-like texture and allows its pure chocolate essence to come shining through. The epitome of sophisticated chocolate desserts, this lovely cake is sure to become a favorite for special occasions.

6 oz. semisweet chocolate of fine quality
6 large eggs, separated
1 tsp. pure vanilla
1 T. strong coffee
5 oz. granulated sugar
2 c. heavy cream (not *ultra-pasteurized,*
     if possible)
6 oz. semisweet chocolate
Kirschwasser
Cocoa

Melt 6 oz. of chocolate and stir into beaten egg yolks. Stir in coffee. In a separate bowl, whip the whites gradually, adding sugar until they form soft peaks. Fold

MUNSON'S CANDY KITCHEN

BOB MUNSON HAS SIX STORES IN THE GREATER CENTRAL CONNECTICUT AREA, AND makes good use of the region's special bounty: strawberries. According to Munson, CT, strawberries are superior due to the high elevation and rocky soil in which they grow. And these luscious berries are even more superior after Munson has dipped them in chocolate. The berries are picked at 7 A.M., destemmed and covered in chocolate at the factory at 8 A.M., and are in Munson's shops by 1 P.M. to be sold and eaten that very day. "Twelve to fourteen hours from stem to stomach," Munson explains. These blissful berries are available only for about three weeks, from Father's Day to the Fourth of July weekend.

All year round, Munson makes excellent butter creams, chocolate bark, and fudge, plus whimsical novelty items. Try the "Chocolate Pizza," manufactured in a real pizza pan with white chocolate standing in nobly for mozzarella cheese, walnuts for pieces of meat, and marshmallows and pecans sprinkled on for added effect. Or how about a chocolate "Wowburger," complete with two chocolate buns, nuts, raisins, and a grain wafer "pickle."

Munson's does a full mail order business (everything except those *half the whites into the chocolate, then fold in the other half.*

Divide the mix into two buttered and floured 2-inch high pans, filling only halfway. Bake at 375° for 15 to 18 minutes. The layers will puff up very high but fall when removed from the oven. Invert the pans on a cooling rack and unmold. Makes two 8-inch layers.

For the filling: Whip the heavy cream, but not until stiff. Melt 6 oz. semisweet chocolate. Add and gently mix into the chocolate one-third of the cream, then fold in the remaining cream.

Place one layer of the cake in a cake pan with parchment on the bottom. Sprinkle the layer with Kirschwasser and add the chocolate whipped cream to form the center layer, reserving some of the cream for the top and some for the sides.

Place the second layer on top of the whipped cream (it should be just below the lip of the pan). Smooth over the top with part of the reserved cream, being sure the surface is extremely smooth. Chill for 4 hours.

Unmold by running a knife around the outside and turn out on parchment. Turn right side up and smooth the sides with remaining cream. Dust the top with sifted cocoa.

delicate berries), and due to thermal packing, can ship even during the warmer months without concern. They will ship to all destinations in the United States and Canada.

OSOGUD CANDIES

THESE HONEST, CHEWY, HAND-DIPPED CHOCOLATES GOT THEIR START OVER FIFTY years ago in the foothills bordering Pasadena, CA, when two European candymakers teamed up to open a shop offering handmade chocolates using high-quality ingredients. Legend has it that one day, a new recipe inspired one of the owners to shout out, "Oh, so good!" Osogud soon became the name for their entire line.

Today, Osogud is still making quality chocolates in healthy American sizes, and if you like big, satisfying mouthfuls of milk chocolate, vanilla-centered peanut clusters, crisp, crunchy English toffee, or generous pecan turtles, you'll probably agree with Osogud's onomatopoeic name.

Visit the shop or write for mail-order information. Orders must be through a wholesaler, and they will ship in the United States and Canada.

PRICE'S FINE CHOCOLATES

PRICE'S CLAIM TO FAME IS ITS "ANNACLAIRS": DAINTY VANILLA CREAM CENTERS, double dipped in a combination of milk or dark chocolate blended with pecans. The piece was designed as a wedding present from Mr. Price to his niece, Annaclair, and now, over seventy years later, we can still enjoy the generosity of his gift.

Price's also makes a large variety of tasty caramels, creams, and nougats, and will present them all to a lucky recipient in "Candy by the Yard," a three-foot-long, almost three pound assortment.

Mail or phone orders are taken for the United States only; write or call for further information.

REGINA LEE'S CANDIES

REGINA LEE'S CANDIES IS A TRADITIONAL OPERATION IN THE BEST SENSE OF THE word. At Regina Lee's, chocolates are entirely handmade: hand rolled,

Chocolate Hunting: What's New in Shops

These days, it is almost impossible to go shopping in a department store without encountering something chocolate. Thus shopping has taken on new attractions for chocolate lovers. While every department store seems to carry the more well-known varieties of chocolate, certain emporiums deserve special mention for their extensive chocolate collections. Among these are: Bloomingdales, whose Au Chocolat boutique sets the standard for what is new, chic, and trendy—as well as tasty—in chocolate; Macy's, whose Cellar is always well stocked with chocolate treats of all nations and all descriptions; Nieman Marcus, with its Texas-sized assortment of chocolate treats; Saks Fifth Avenue, which stocks truffles, fruits de mer (gorgeous chocolate seashells), and luscious chocolate assortments; and Marshall Fields, whose "Frango Mints" are perennial favorites.

The gourmet food shop, specializing in exotic edibles of all types, naturally does not neglect the world of chocolate. Among these noteworthy additions to chocolate supply are New York City's Balducci's, DDL Foodshow, Dean and DeLuca, Faye and Allen's Foodworks, and Zabar's. However, while New York City does seem to hand cut, and hand coated. The only machine on the premises is a cream beater, says candymaker Bill Yeager.

Among the best offerings are a melt-in-your-mouth peanut butter fluff covered in chocolate, icy green-and-white chocolate mints, and a sweetly chewable milk chocolate–covered vanilla caramel. Regina Lee's also prepares a complete line of chocolate creams, fruits, and nuts.

Prices range from $5.25 to $7.25 per pound, and Regina Lee's will ship its all-American goodies all over the world.

REGINA'S FINE CANDIES

REGINA'S IS A FAMILY OPERATION OVER FIFTY YEARS OLD. THE ELLIOT FAMILY PRIDES itself on quality ingredients, such as hand-cracked California walnuts, sweet cream butter, and real whipping cream. The fine quality assorted candies are still cooked in traditional copper kettles and made on old-fashioned marble tables. After all, says Mike Elliot, third-generation candymaker, "Grandma's name is on every box. Naturally, we exercise a lot of control and care."

lead the way, you don't have to be a Manhattanite to find excellent selections of chocolate in your own area. Gourmet food shops are burgeoning all over the United States and Canada, and when they arrive, the aroma of chocolate is never far behind.

Lastly, perhaps the most uplifting news of all for chocolate lovers is that chocolate shops are becoming more elegant and inventive by the minute. No longer must you be satisfied with banal assortments of overly familiar varieties in dusty boxes. Nowadays, what is available in the new wave of chocolate shops is far more unique and exciting. Like so much else, innovation in chocolate shops seems centered in the California area. Two in the forefront of this trend are San Francisco's Confetti and Beverly Hills' Chocolat du Monde. These shops will sell their precious wares by the piece, which will enable even the most finicky connoisseur to create the ultimate assortment.

By necessity, the above information can only serve as a limited guide for the resourceful chocolate consumer. The world of chocolate is changing—thankfully, always for the better, but so rapidly that it has become almost impossible to document it. The best advice one can offer is to keep shopping and scouting, and to follow your nose toward that special, intoxicating aroma of chocolate. Happy hunting and happy eating.

The care is evident in Regina's chewy "Pecanettes," in which top-quality whole pecans are covered with a whipped cream caramel and dipped in dark chocolate; and the chocolate-dipped apricots, tart and of an altogether satisfying texture—a substantial, healthy-tasting treat. Also noteworthy are Mike Elliot's favorite: "Mike's Mints." ("My family will say I'm tooting my own horn, but they really are good," Mike claims.) Indeed, Mike's Mints are cool and refreshing, and their contrasting colors of brown and green make them pleasing to the eye as well as the palate.

Regina's has five stores in the Minneapolis-St. Paul area, and will gladly fill mail and phone orders in the United States only. Prices range from $7.50 to $12.50 a pound, depending on the assortment.

ROCCOCO CHOCOLATES

IF YOU'RE A CONFIRMED TRUFFLE FIEND, YOU OWE IT TO YOURSELF TO VISIT Portland, OR, where Roccoco Chocolates is creating top-of-the-line truffle masterpieces. These truffles are special because of the incredible amount of tender loving care that goes into creating each one. They are completely handmade in small batches from start to finish, a process that includes hand dipping and even hand tempering. Add to all that attention such impeccable ingredients as Guittard chocolate, which creates a special coating for each Roccoco truffle that is shiny and properly "snappy," marvelous fillings, and real liquors and liqueurs (Oregon has recently legalized the inclusion of alcohol in chocolates), with nary a preservative nor artificial flavor in sight, and the result is truffle heaven.

Among the most memorable flavors are an excellent "Raspberry Truffle," which is deep, dark, and subtle, with real seeds evident to the bite. Its dark chocolate exterior is artfully swirled with decorative white chocolate squiggles. The "Apricot Truffle" has an intriguing tangy center, sparked by appealing apricot flecks. The "Orange Almond Truffle" is an impressive combination of two grownup flavors that work extra magic together. Also notable are Roccoco's delicious "Grand Marnier," "Amaretto Traditional" (which makes good use of Amaretto di Saronno liqueur), and refreshing "French Truffle Mint."

These chocolates are available in several other Oregon locations. The shop will accept mail orders to the United States and Canada, but, as truffles are fragile and alcohol-containing products may not be sent outside state lines, you may decide that a trip to the American Northwest is in order.

RONSVALLE'S

GLADYS RONSVALLE HAS BEEN MAKING CHOCOLATES FOR OVER FIFTY YEARS, AND she still does all the "little tiny things," (like making the same smooth fondant that tastes like heavy whipping cream), that have made her candy business such a big success.

A Ronsvalle assortment has a wonderful homemade look, with small, delicate pieces that encourage you to sample more—and more. The chocolate is creamy and not overly sweet, and it covers pleasantly chewy raisins and dates to perfection. Ronsvalle's is famous for its "Chippies": tiny pieces of potato chip, coated with chocolate and made into surprisingly tasty patties. But for more traditional tastes, you can't go wrong with Ronsvalle's dark chocolates with strawberry cream centers, or their milk chocolate with walnut.

Prices are a reasonable $7 per pound. Ronsvalle's will fill mail orders all over North America, and, Gladys Ronsvalle assures, to every continent in the world.

THE SAN FRANCISCO CHOCOLATE COMPANY

THE GINSBURGS, WHO OWN AND RUN THE SAN FRANCISCO CHOCOLATE COMPANY, ARE relative newcomers to the world of chocolate making. They were enthusiastic chocolate lovers who knew all about how to eat it, and had definite opinions about what types of chocolate they liked, but did not know how to prepare it. However, an educated palate is the first key to successful chocolate making, as the Ginsburgs soon learned. They obtained recipes from Belgium and Germany, and began to experiment with creating their own chocolates. The results are now bringing joy to California chocolate lovers.

The Ginsburgs make superb truffles, using Callebaut couverture for the outer shells and Guittard chocolate plus lots of butter and cream for the ganache filling. They then add special flavors, such as Chambord liqueur, which imparts a subtle raspberry taste that enhances, rather than competes with, the chocolate, and Bailey's Irish Cream liqueur, whose rich and mellow taste adds even more smoothness to the chocolate truffle plush.

The San Francisco Chocolate Company has also created a delicious new concoction which they have termed the "Truffwich." This is a devilishly addictive sandwich of two slim wafers filled with ganache and dipped into chocolate—something any chocoholic would look forward to finding in his or her lunchbox!

Visit the San Francisco Chocolate Company's shop in person, or contact them for information about mailing their delicious chocolate specialties to you, whether you live in the United States or Canada.

STORK'S
PASTRY SHOP

THE STORK FAMILY MAKES ITS DELIGHTFUL CHOCOLATES AND PASTRIES FRESH DAILY. Their chocolate couverture is imported Belgian Callebaut, and they use pure butter, cream, and imported liquor—never a preservative nor an artificial ingredient.

Stork's *"Escargots,"* or chocolate snail shells, are molded in milk chocolate and striped in dark chocolate, then filled with a splendid praline paste that is an inspired blend of hazelnuts, almonds, and macadamias. Stork's "Irish Coffee Truffles" are velvety, deep, and dark. Stork's "Cat's Tongues" in milk or dark chocolate are pretty and dainty, with cat's faces embossed on each end. These are a perfect gift for the cat-loving chocolate fan.

"Baumkuchen," a Stork specialty, is a light, airy cake baked on a rotisserie, layer by individual layer. Each layer is coated with chocolate, and the result is a beautiful tree-trunk effect. The *Baumkuchen* is cut into cubes before eating, and every bite is a pleasure.

Stork's prices range from $10.50 a pound for *Baumkuchen,* $16.00 a pound for assorted chocolates, and $19.00 a pound for the *Escargots,* because of the extra labor involved in their production.

Stork's chocolates are sold at Macy's and Balducci's in New York, as well as at various hotels around the country. If you cannot visit their Queens bakery, write or call for a location near you. They accept mail and telephone orders and will send chocolates anywhere in North America.

THE SWEET SHOP

THE SWEET SHOP'S HAND-DIPPED DELICACIES, WHICH ARE FREE OF PRESERVATIVES, and all made with an abundance of real whipping cream and butter, fresh whole milk, chocolate liquor, and cocoa butter, can be found in Neiman Marcus, the Belk Department Stores, and Saks Fifth Avenue. But up till now you probably didn't know it, because these mouth-watering pieces are sold as the "house brand," not under their own name.

But Sweet Shop chocolates by any name are delicious—particularly their number one best-seller, the "Fudge Love": a creamy cocoa-redolent fudgy center, dipped in milk or dark chocolate with pecans. The Sweet Shop is also the originator of the "American Truffle," a huge, Texas-sized morsel with the dark, rich taste of "Swiss Mint," "Irish Mocha," or "Texas Cocoa."

These chocolates retail for between $12 and $15 per pound. You can pick up the pride of the Lone Star State at Neiman Marcus, or contact the manufacturer for a location near you. They will take mail and telephone orders, but they ship only in the cooler months.

SWEET SWISS

CONFISEUR JOE NENDL LEARNED THE CANDY BUSINESS IN SWITZERLAND, AND HAS practiced his art in the United States for thirty-four years. "You have to live in it, devote all your time to it, and take no shortcuts," he declares. But the results are worth his trouble. Nendl's candies are genuine European works of art—lovely "Mandarin Marzipan," "Cointreau Cups," and champagne and rum truffles, for example. The "Coffee Rum Brazil," with its smooth rum flavor, is a particular favorite, as are the coconut pecan and the amaretto truffle.

Nendl's ingredients come from all over the world: Callebaut chocolate couverture from Belgium, French champagne extract for his truffles, Italian Amorino cherries for his cordials.

It all adds up to international chocolate good cheer. Luckily, from his one little shop in Spokane, Nendl ships his specialties wholesale to forty states, as well as to Puerto Rico and Australia. Write or call to find out where Sweet Swiss chocolates are available near you. They accept mail and telephone orders from Canada, too.

THAT'S MY FAVORITE

FORMER MODEL AND ACTRESS CATHY GOLDSTEIN MAKES JUST ONE CANDY: CHOCO-late almond buttercrunch. And when you succumb to this crunchy, buttery, chocolatey stuff, you might agree with Goldstein's appellation.

Gaily packaged in dayglo pink and electric blue and sealed in shiny silver foil for freshness, these crunchy candies make quite an impression. At $16 per pound, they are pricey, but if this sort of candy is your favorite, who cares about price?

That's My Favorite is available at such department stores as Jordan Marsh, Macy's, and Neiman Marcus. Goldstein will fill mail orders from the United States and Canada, except during the summer months.

VALENTINE'S COSMOPOLITAN CONFECTIONS
～✠～

VALENTINE'S ELEGANT CHOCOLATES ARE SOMETHING OF A FAMILY TRADITION. DARIA Baranhoff's Russian grandfather started a highly successful confectionery shop in the unlikely locale of Kobe, Japan. Today, her father and brother have shops in several Japanese cities, and they still make their own chocolate couverture in their Kobe factory. Here in California, Daria uses her family's Japanese-made chocolate, which is refined continuously between stone conches for fourteen days, to make her own special delights, such as the "Marinco Truffle" (named for Marin County, CA), flavored with orange liqueur and rolled in almonds; the "Plum and Crême" a plump prune covered with cream and dark chocolate; and three types of homemade fudge.

Visit the shop, or order by mail or phone to receive these sweet Valentines. Whether you're in Kobe, California, or Canada, you'll just fall in love with these treats.

LA VIOLETTE CHOCOLATIER
～✠～

MRS. ANGELA KOSUBAL LEARNED CHOCOLATE MAKING IN AUSTRIA. SHE TAUGHT HER daughters, Natalie and Angela, the art, and the three (luckily for us) decided to open their own shop and share their Old-World expertise with the public.

"We make everything ourselves," says Mrs. Kosubal. "There are no machines, no conveyor belts in our shop. We taste everything, because we know what tastes good to us will taste good to others."

The Kosubals pride themelves on not making "sweet sweets," preferring to let people taste the flavor of the chocolate and the contrast it makes with its fruit or nut filling. Thus raspberries are zesty and tart, a fitting foil for their dark, creamy chocolate coating. The walnut cream, fudgy, smooth, and meltingly delicious, is a winner, as is the artful dark or white chocolate almond bark, with its appealing nutty freshness and snap.

La Violette's novelty items are extensive. Daughter Natalie is a first-rate chocolate artist, who can re-create even the most detailed and elaborately illustrated wine labels in chocolate, as well as the occasional pet horse, Rolls Royce, Ferrari, running shoe, or portrait of a favorite rock star. "I encourage people to talk to me and tell me about themselves before I make something for them," Natalie says. "That way I can really get the feel of what they want. And so many customers have become our friends."

The Kosubals carry chocolate-making equipment for those who want to try their hand at home, but with all these delights ready-made, you may not feel inspired to do anything more than reach for another bite.

Prices are $14 a pound for an assortment. At this time, La Violette does not fill mail orders, but if there is enough of a demand, perhaps they could be convinced.

WILBUR
CHOCOLATE COMPANY, INC.

WILBUR HAS BEEN MAKING CHOCOLATE SINCE 1884: THE SWEET LITTLE MORSELS called "Wilbur Buds," which resemble (and predate) Hershey's kisses, tasty chocolate bars for munching and baking, and Dutch process cocoa, among other items. All are delicious and have a uniquely American flavor—the kind of candy we remember from "the good old days."

Wilbur ages the chocolate liquor it uses in its Wilbur Buds to bring out more of the chocolate flavor. In fact, Wilbur Buds may contain chunks of bittersweet chocolate a full ten years old!

Wilbur makes what many consider the best American chocolate bars. Both their "dark sweet" and milk chocolate bars are thick and creamy, solid and substantial.

Wilbur chocolates are available in department stores around the United States, or write or call the company in Lititz, PA. Unfortunately, they only ship in the United States. If you ever happen to be in Lititz, be sure to visit Wilbur's "Candy Americana Museum." The Wilbur people know their chocolate.

YUGOSLAVIA

JOSIP KRAS

KRAS IS ONE OF THE OLDEST, AND BEST, PREWAR CHOCOLATE COMPANIES IN YUGO-slavia. Although the bulk of Kras's business is prepackaging chocolates for other companies (even some products for Tobler, they tell us), Kras also produces commendable chocolates for export under its own name. The liquid-centered chocolate cherry cordials are delicious, with a strong and piquant cherry flavor. And the Kras "liquor-filled" bonbons (which manage to pass muster in the United States due to their less than 1.5 percent alcohol content) are a thoroughly enjoyable way to familiarize oneself with Balkan chocolate.

Another pleasing thing about Josip Kras is its prices: from $2.95 to $6.95 for a box of bonbons! Ample reason to seek out Kras chocolates and give the name the following it deserves. Contact Tina, Son, & Co. for more information or visit your local specialty shop.

How to Conduct a Chocolate Tasting

NOW THAT YOU KNOW HOW TO SELECT FINE CHOCOLATES, YOU'RE READY FOR ONE OF the most pleasurable rituals ever devised—a chocolate tasting. This event is similar to a wine tasting, but with an obvious advantage. The aim is to learn which chocolates you like best and why. This last bit of information will be invaluable on future chocolate expeditions.

Don't attempt to sample more than a half dozen or so different chocolates at one sitting. Otherwise, the tastes begin to run into one another and you will not be able to discern the more subtle differences in each chocolate. Better to have several different sittings at different times.

Pick chocolates that have something in common, so that you will have certain traits to compare. For example, you could limit yourself to chocolates from one country, such as Belgium or Switzerland, or to different dark chocolates, chocolate-covered cherries, chocolate bars, or that most exalted of chocolate confections—the truffle.

Use a sharp knife to cut each chocolate in half. You will then be able to examine how each piece is made. With filled chocolates, the more elegant pieces will have a thin and delicate bottom rather than a thick one. Next see whether you can discern distinct layers of filling.

When tasting, go slowly. Allow each sample to melt on your tongue, and try to think about what flavors predominate in each. Clear your palate after each sample with cognac or white wine, or, if you must, plain water.

When you have found one manufacturer that is a clear winner, you might then want to plan a tasting around chocolates made solely by that manufacturer, thus determining which pieces you believe are the best of the best.

One final hint: although it is undeniably pleasant to keep all the chocolate one wants to oneself, a chocolate tasting is even better with company. Others' opinions may be invaluable in helping you to ascertain just what a particular flavor is, or to pinpoint why a certain chocolate is preferred universally. Just be sure that there is more than enough of everything to go around. There is nothing worse than a chocolate tasting ending in a "hung jury" as a result of insufficient evidence.

Care, Storage, and Freezing of Chocolate

CHOCOLATE, LIKE MOST THINGS OF VALUE, RESPONDS BEST TO TENDER, LOVING care. Fragile pieces, such as truffles or bonbons with crème fraîche filling, must be eaten on the same day purchased, or as close to that date as possible (which is what usually happens, anyway), in order to experience them at their peak. However, most chocolates, even those that do not contain preservatives, are capable of lasting far longer than you might expect. For example, milk chocolate has a shelf life of about six to eight months, and dark chocolate may be kept as long as eighteen months to two years—and sometimes even longer for both. This is true, however, only if you store them correctly.

To keep chocolates in optimum condition, they must be stored *unopened.* Keep them in a cool, dry place away from heat or direct sunlight—usually a kitchen cupboard or cabinet. Ideally, the temperature inside should range from fifty-five to sixty-five degrees Fahrenheit, and should never be allowed to exceed seventy degrees; relative humidity (should you be equipped to measure such things in your home) should be about fifty percent, and should never exceed sixty-five percent. This means that the storage cupboard or cabinet should not feel at all damp. Also, since chocolate functions like a blotter when it encounters strong smells, it should never be left near substances with aggressive aromas.

The reason for such stringent temperature control is that unattractive enemy of chocolatedom, "bloom." During wide variations in temperature (which often occur during the summer months), some of the cocoa butter in chocolate tends to melt and then reharden, causing a distinct whitish or grayish film to appear on the chocolate's surface. Bloom does not really harm the chocolate, in that it only slightly affects taste and certainly will not make you ill. But bloom is unappetizing to behold and, since it can be avoided relatively easily, should not have to compromise your chocolate-eating experience.

Many people mistakenly believe that the refrigerator is the best storehouse for any chocolate not consumed after opening the box. But refrigeration tends to do chocolate more harm than good. When refrigerated, chocolate will collect an unsightly film of moisture on its surface. It will also pick up the smells of whatever is alongside it. So unless you want soggy chocolates that are unpleasantly reminiscent of yesterday's camembert or smoked salmon, keep them out of the fridge. However, if you feel you absolutely must refrigerate, first take the precaution of wrapping the chocolate in foil, then placing it in a plastic bag, and finally, in an airtight container—this, at least, should prevent the odor problem. And remember, if you do refrigerate your chocolates, to allow them time to soften and come back to room temperature before you serve them.

There is another, far superior, alternative to refrigerating chocolates, and that is freezing them. Before the summer, when many of the finer chocolate shops go on vacation, savvy chocolate lovers stock up on quantities of their favorite pieces, taking advantage of this "cold storage" method so that they need suffer no deprivation nor be bereft of bonbons during the dog days of August. Freezing is also the method of choice for extras from a box that has already been opened.

Skeptics will be pleasantly surprised to find just how well this seemingly unorthodox method works. You must be sure to wrap each individual piece of chocolate well in aluminum foil before placing it in the freezer. Then, remember to take the chocolate out a day before you plan to serve it, to allow it to return to room temperature. Do not, however, unwrap the chocolate until it has thawed and serving is imminent.

A cautionary note: Once chocolates have thawed, they should not be refrozen. You'll simply have to eat them all.

Cooking with Chocolate

AS WONDERFUL AS CHOCOLATE IS WHEN EATEN ON ITS OWN, IT CAN BE EVEN MORE spectacular when combined with other top-quality ingredients. Thus, cooking with chocolate as the main ingredient affords a special pleasure.

After trying your hand at brownies, cookies, and cakes, you probably already know something about chocolate cookery. But have you ever been disappointed by any of your efforts? Most of us, for example, have suffered through at least one batch of brownies that had an inexplicably burnt aroma, or icings that tasted more of sugar than chocolate, or cake that was dry and crumbly rather than properly moist and fudgy. The following hints about cooking with chocolate should enable you to use that most valuable—and volatile—of ingredients to its best advantage in all your future dessert creations.

Before discussing how to handle the chocolate, it is important to mention the first rule of anyone who is serious about using it: always buy the best. Supermarkets are full of what is called "baking chocolate," which is generally, whether unsweetened or semisweet, not of the highest quality. This undistinguished chocolate's sole virtues are its low price and wide availability. However, it is worthwhile to become discriminating about the quality of chocolate you use in your baking and cooking. Especially with chocolate, the better the raw material, the better the finished product. If you aren't convinced, try tasting some of the semisweet "baking chocolate" you probably have in your cupboard right now. Not exactly appetizing, is it? In contrast, the following types of semisweet baking chocolate are all delicious enough to eat on their own—which should tell you a great deal about what they will do for your baking: Maillard "Eagle Sweet Chocolate"; Wilbur "Dark Sweet Chocolate; Lindt *"Surfin"* and *"Excellence"*; Tobler *"Extra Bittersweet"* and *"Tradition"*; Cailler *"Crémant"*; and Sarotti *"Edel Bitter."* If, however, you need an unsweetened chocolate, you might want to try using the following excellent varieties: Callebaut Unsweetened; Wilbur Gourmet Baking Bar; and World's Finest Baking Chocolate. (All of these can be ordered from Madame Chocolate, 1940–C Lehigh Avenue, Glenview, IL 60025, or try other chocolate suppliers you are familiar with.) Because these three were intended originally for professional bakers, they are available in larger quantities than you may be accustomed to working with. The Callebaut comes in an eleven-pound (five kilo) block, the Wilbur in a five-pound block, and the World's Finest in a sixteen-ounce bar. But, properly stored chocolate has a long shelf life (see "Care, Storage, and Freezing of Chocolate," p. 99), so keeping the excess in top condition is not really a problem.

If a recipe calls for unsweetened chocolate but you would prefer to use a semisweetened variety, you should have no trouble doing so. Just add a bit more chocolate and somewhat less sugar than indicated.

101

Now that you've chosen your chocolate, here is some advice on how to work with it. Many experienced chocolate chefs prefer to work in a cool room (under sixty-five degrees Fahrenheit is best) so that the volatile chocolate does not begin to melt before it should.

As for the melting itself, there are many theories on how it should be accomplished. Many chefs swear by that old standby, the double boiler (or, if you do not possess such an appliance, an improvised one consisting of a regular saucepan that fits comfortably atop a pan of boiling water). However, just as many others seem to feel that the high heat of a double boiler may scorch the chocolate, rendering it grainy and difficult to use. They prefer alternate methods, such as: placing the chocolate in a pan and putting it in an oven with a pilot light overnight, which will guarantee melted chocolate the next morning; or placing the pan of chocolate atop a warming tray or "hot tray," designed to keep food warm at a relatively low temperature. Some chefs opt for melting the chocolate in a pan, either by itself or with other ingredients such as butter and sugar (if the recipe calls for this), directly over a low flame, stirring constantly. If you are melting the chocolate by itself, it may help to grate a portion of it first, taking advantage of the scientific principle that breaking down an object and thus adding to its surface area will cause it to melt more quickly. Or, if you have a microwave oven, you might want to put space-age technology to work—this timesaver will miraculously melt your chocolate in thirty seconds!

Whatever method you use to melt your chocolate, be careful not to let any stray drops of water get into the mixture, because they will cause the chocolate to stiffen and thicken. For the same reason, never cover chocolate that is melting or has already melted—steam will collect on the lid, quickly condensing into water and falling into the chocolate. Similarly, all utensils which will come into contact with the chocolate should be kept absolutely dry.

Finally, if in some capricious mood you decide you must cook "something chocolate," but find that your larder is bare of all but cocoa, not to worry. Three tablespoons of cocoa plus one tablespoon of shortening may be pressed into service to substitute for a one-ounce square of unsweetened baking chocolate. The taste will not be exactly the same, but the finished product should still assuage your chocolate cravings nicely, fortifying you enough to get to the store and replenish your chocolate supply.

Note: For hints on decorating your finished chocolate creations with—what else?—more chocolate, turn to "Hints on Chocolate Shaping" on the following page.

Hints on Chocolate Shaping

Nothing gives desserts more panache than the professional touch garnered from real chocolate decorations. Artfully positioned chocolate curls and shavings will lend a pastry-shop polish to your creations, and what's more, they are easy and fun to make. The following tips should give you the idea.

Chocolate shavings are the simplest to make, so novices might want to start with them. First chill your chocolate (this is one instance when the refrigerator becomes a friend rather than an enemy of chocolate) for about an hour prior to use, so that you have a solid block that will not melt and gum up the works. Now, simply grate until you have the desired amount. A hand-held rotary grater (such as is used to grate hard cheeses) is ideal for making shavings, but you can also use a regular grater held over a bowl large enough to catch every shaving. Or, if you have a food processor, you may use the metal blade, first being sure that the chocolate is soft enough to be pierced easily by a sharp knife. Cut the chocolate into pieces small enough to be dropped through the feed tube and run until chocolate is grated to desired fineness (this will give you very fine, delicate shavings).

Chocolate curls are a particularly attractive garnish to cakes, mousses, parfaits, etc. Luckily, they are far more impressive to look at than they are difficult to prepare. To make chocolate curls, start with semisweet or extra bittersweet chocolate that has been left out in a warm room and allowed to reach about eighty degrees Fahrenheit (the chocolate will splinter if it is too cold). Then, using a potato peeler, vegetable parer, or small, sharp knife, "shave" the chocolate. Work with the utensil, always moving lengthwise, to get long, well-defined curls. It is important to use long, smooth strokes and thin slices, as these will produce the most impressive specimens.

Swiss Almond Mousse Parfait

(Created for Lindt of Switzerland by Joe Baumer, chef of Baumer & Crooks Restaurant Corp., New York, NY.)

This luscious chocolate almond mousse will provide a delicious and elegant end to any special dinner. What's more, it is remarkably simple to prepare.

> 6 oz. Lindt Swiss dark chocolate
>   (or other Swiss dark chocolate)
> ¼ c. rum
> ¼ c. orange juice
> ½ c. ground salted almonds
> 2 egg yolks
> 2 whole eggs
> ½ c. sugar
> ½ pint heavy cream, whipped

Melt the chocolate slowly in the rum and orange juice. Grind the almonds in a blender or food processor. Add almonds to chocolate and stir. Set aside to cool. Put the egg yolks, whole eggs, and sugar in a mixer and beat until light and fluffy. Add the chocolate mixture, fold together until smooth, then fold in the whipped cream. Pour into a bowl or individual parfait glasses. Freeze for several hours.
Serves 4.

International Chocolate Fondue

Fondue, which literally means "melted" in French, is an especially congenial dessert for chocolate lovers the world over. Be sure to provide toothpicks, skewers, or long forks for dipping.

8 oz. Belgian, German, or Swiss
    bittersweet chocolate
8 oz. Swiss or Dutch milk chocolate
¾ c. light cream or half-and-half
3 T. Kahlua, Triple Sec, or Amaretto
    liqueur
For dipping: small chunks of pound or
    sponge cake and fresh fruit (whole
    strawberries or cherries, orange
    segments, and chunks of pineapple,
    apple, pear, or banana

Break up chocolate into small chunks. Combine chocolate chunks with cream or half-and-half in heavy saucepan or electric fondue pot. Stir often over low heat until mixture is melted and very smooth. Immediately before serving, stir in liqueur of choice. Serve with cake and/or fruit.
Serves 8.

Drinking Chocolate

A STEAMING, FROTHY CUP OF COCOA IS ONE OF THE WORLD'S GREAT RESTORATIVES. If you view cocoa as a humble beverage that is strictly nursery fare, you are doing both it and yourself a great disservice. The preservative-packed, presweetened, chalky stuff so often confused with cocoa is not really cocoa at all, but an anemic concoction called by the euphemistic, neither-here-nor-there term, "chocolate drink." True cocoa is unsweetened, and preparing it requires a bit more elbow grease. However, cocoa's richly aromatic rewards are worth your time and effort.

To make a superior cup of cocoa, it is necessary to start with the best possible ingredients. Many chocolate drinkers prefer hot chocolate that has been "dutched," that is, cocoa powder to which an alkali such as potassium or sodium bicarbonate has been added, in order to neutralize the cocoa bean's natural acidity. Van Houten and Droste, both products of the Netherlands' cocoa know-how, make particularly fine examples of this type of Dutch chocolate.

But you don't necessarily have to go Dutch to get delicious cocoa. Other excellent cocoas that will produce a more than creditable cup are Switzerland's Cailler, France's Poulain, and the American favorites, Wilbur's Ideal Cocoa and Hershey's.

Once you've selected your cocoa, your first step is to prepare a cocoa paste. Add sugar to taste (proportions vary according to personal preference, but to make one cup you might begin by trying a teaspoon of cocoa with one and one-half to two teaspoons sugar to start), plus a small amount of the liquid of your choice—preferably cream or milk or a mixture of the two, but water is acceptable if you're feeling Spartan—in order to moisten the mixture. The paste should then be stirred over low heat until all ingredients are blended and smooth.

The remaining milk or cream should then be added, and the mixture stirred continuously until heated through. Just before the cocoa would come to a boil, remove the pan from the heat and continue to stir, using a wire whisk or beater, until the mixture is frothy. This final step prevents any milky skin from forming and also serves to bring out the full cocoa flavor.

At last, the cocoa is ready to grace your favorite mug. It may be further glamorized with a topping of fresh whipped cream and cinnamon (in the Viennese manner), or a dash of spirits (for that après-ski feeling). If you feel as if you could profit from a bit of babying, add some marshmallows to the finished product and voilà—one cup of instant well-being. (Think of it as chicken soup with a college education.)

Although drinking chocolate these days generally means cocoa, to Central and South Americans and Spaniards the words have a more literal meaning. In these cultures, which were the cradle of chocolate civilization, drinking chocolate signifies just that: real, unsweetened chocolate. To make your own facsimile of this noble nectar, start with a

Chocolate Liqueurs

Chocolate liqueurs are an ideal compromise for adults who remember their cocoa and marshmallow days fondly, but now prefer to satisfy their taste for chocolate drinks in a zestier, more spirited manner. As is true with eating chocolate, chocolate liqueurs are made of a blend of cocoa beans, roasted for a particular length of time according to secret recipes. The beans are then blended with vanilla and spirits, and with other flavorings, to make a worthy potion that is either chocolate brown in color or colorless. Crème de cacao is the simplest and most well known chocolate liqueur. Among the best available varieties are Leroux, Hiram Walker, and Marie Brizzard.

A bit more complex than crème de cacao are the chocolate cordial combinations, which add another flavor, such as almonds, cherries, mint, citrus fruits, coco-

chunk of plain unsweetened chocolate (about one ounce for one cup). To make your drink authentic, you might want to try using a Puerto Rican brand of chocolate such as Cortés or Goya, or the Mexican brands Ibarra or El Molino. Combine this chocolate with honey or sugar to taste (about one and one-half to two teaspoons) plus a pinch of cinammon and nutmeg, and a small amount of water. Melt the mixture over a double boiler or over very low heat, stirring almost continuously. When all ingredients are blended, add a mixture of one-half cup of milk and one-half cup of cream, and stir till just before the mixture would come to a *nut, or coffee to the potent chocolate brew. Examples are Hiram Walker's chocolate mint, chocolate cherry, and Swiss chocolate almond; as well as many international varieties, such as Israel's Sabra (a blend of chocolate and Jaffa oranges), Switzerland's Cheri-Suisse (which combines chocolate with cherries), and Holland's Vandermint (in which the sparkle of mint spices up the chocolate).*

The newest category in the chocolate liqueur family is the cream liqueurs, in which cream is brought into the blend of chocolate and spirits, imparting a pleasingly smooth richness to the brew. The top of the line include Droste's Cream Liqueur, Leroux's Irish Cream, and Bailey's Original Irish Cream. All are quite a step up from plain milk and chocolate.

These drinks may all be savored on their own, on the rocks, as a flavorful addition to postprandial coffee, or poured over ice cream for a truly special sundae.

boil. Remove it from the heat and, using a wire whisk or beater (or, to be truly authentic, a Mexican chocolate mill called a *molinillo,* which can sometimes be purchased at the stores that carry Mexican chocolate), beat until foamy. For an even thicker, richer, and more sustaining drink, you might try beating an egg yolk into the mixture after it has been removed from the heat. When you have perfected your own version of *chocolatl,* you will surely understand why the Spaniards were so reluctant to share this spicily sensuous, warm brew with anyone else. Luckily for us, though, the secret is out.

Sources

CANADA

Alberta

RETAILERS

CHOCOLATE CHOCOLAT
D207 West Edmonton Mall
Edmonton, Alberta
(403) 487-682

CHOCOLATE GOURMET TREATS
43 Kingsway Garden Mall
Edmonton, Alberta
(403) 479-2317

PALACE OF SWEETS
57A Meadowlark Park Shopping Centre
Edmonton, Alberta
(403) 489-8537

SWEET HUT
13 Deer Valley Centre
Calgary, Alberta
(403) 278-2002

SWEETS & TREATS
9114 112th Street
Edmonton, Alberta
(403) 433-4929

TOUTE SWEET
880 16th Avenue, SW
Calgary, Alberta
(403) 264-3067

MANUFACTURERS & DISTRIBUTORS

HAWKINS & COMPANY FUDGE & FANCIES LTD.
115 Heritage Mall
Edmonton, Alberta
(403) 435-0794

LAURA SECORD CANDY SHOPS
Calgary Market Mall
Calgary, Alberta
(403) 286-3445

68 Edmonton Centre
Edmonton, Alberta
(403) 425-8873

R.C. PURDY CHOCOLATES LTD.
Calgary Market Mall
3625 Shaganappi Terrace, NW
Calgary, Alberta
(403) 286-1122

RENAISSANCE CHOCOLATES & CANDIES
14 2439 54th Avenue SW
Calgary, Alberta
(403) 243-3788

British Columbia

RETAILERS

BAIN'S CHOCOLATES & CANDIES
2404 Main Street
Vancouver, British Columbia
(604) 876-5833

BRUSSELS CHOCOLATES LTD.
2257 West 41st Street
Vancouver, British Columbia
(604) 263-3292

CHARLIE'S CHOCOLATE FACTORY LTD.
102-12 Water Street
Vancouver, British Columbia
(604) 688-7333

PAULINE JOHNSON CANDIES
1836 East Hastings Street
Vancouver, British Columbia
(604) 254-9484

R.C. PURDY CHOCOLATES LTD.
2777 Kingsway
Vancouver, British Columbia
(604) 430-6444

TEMPTATIONS CHOCOLATE LTD.
1391 East 33rd Street
Vancouver, British Columbia
(604) 879-8118

TOUT SWEET CHOCOLATES LTD.
332 Water Street
Vancouver, British Columbia
(604) 687-0580

WELCH'S CANDY SHOPS
1840 East Hastings
Vancouver, British Columbia
(604) 255-2601
(mail orders and inquiries)

WILLIAM NEILSON LTD.
7018 14th Avenue
Burnaby, British Columbia
(604) 524-4971

MANUFACTURERS & DISTRIBUTORS

AU CHOCOLAT
1962 West 4th Avenue
Vancouver, British Columbia
(604) 734-4737

LE CHOCOLAT BELGE DANIEL LTD.
1133 Robson Street
Vancouver, British Columbia
(604) 688-9624

DEAN'S CHOCOLATES LTD.
7621 Vantage Way
Delta, British Columbia
(604) 946-1116

Lansdowne Park Shopping Centre
Vancouver, British Columbia
(604) 270-4214

LAURA SECORD CANDY SHOPS
2138 West 41st Street
Vancouver, British Columbia
(604) 263-7216

TEMPTATIONS CHOCOLATE LTD.
5478 Moreland Street
Vancouver, British Columbia
(604) 298-4550

Manitoba

RETAILERS

CANDY CASTLE
1295 Jefferson Street
Winnipeg, Manitoba
(204) 633-7897

CHOCOLATE CHOCOLAT
Eaton Place
Winnipeg, Manitoba
(204) 943-9119

THE CHOCOLATE SHOP
268 Portage Street
Winnipeg, Manitoba
(204) 942-4855

HATFIELD HOUSE SWEET SHOPPE
696 Osborne Street
Winnipeg, Manitoba
(204) 452-9547

TIMBERLAND CONFECTIONERY
9th and Hogan Streets
The Pas, Manitoba
(204) 623-6395

TOWN CONFECTIONERY
184 Kelsey Street
Churchill, Manitoba
(204) 675-2228

MANUFACTURERS & DISTRIBUTORS

DETERS CONFECTIONERY LTD.
235 Fischer
The Pas, Manitoba
(204) 623-2044

LAURA SECORD CANDY SHOPS
Kildonan Place Shopping Centre
Winnipeg, Manitoba
(204) 688-6244

Nova Scotia

RETAILERS

ATLANTIC CANDY LTD.
Pontac House
Halifax, Nova Scotia
(902) 429-6987

CANDY BOWL
6466 Quinpool Road
Halifax, Nova Scotia
(902) 429-8828

ROSE BOWL CANDY SHOP
5692 Spring Garden Road
Halifax, Nova Scotia
(902) 429-9485

SWEET BOUTIQUE
Bayers Road Shopping Centre
Halifax, Nova Scotia
(902) 455-9373

SYBIL'S SWEETS
70 First Lake Drive
Sackville, Nova Scotia
(902) 865-7228

MANUFACTURERS & DISTRIBUTORS

B & M CHOCOLATE CRAFTS
58 Hornes Road
Halifax, Nova Scotia
(902) 469-7228

LAURA SECORD CANDY SHOPS
Micmac Mall
Halifax, Nova Scotia
(902) 963-0155

Ontario

RETAILERS

BOOKS & CHOCOLATES
584 Parliament Street
Toronto, Ontario
(416) 927-0074

CANDY CORNER
Lincoln Fields Plaza
Ottawa, Ontario
(416) 829-8307

CHOCOLATE CHOCOLAT
460 Eglinton West
Toronto, Ontario
(416) 483-7165

CHOCOLATE FANTASIES
1132 Yonge Street
Toronto, Ontario
(416) 924-8640

CHOCOLATE GOURMET TREATS
Billings Bridge Plaza
Ottawa, Ontario
(416) 526-1513

CHOCOLATE SQUIRREL INC.
2460 Yonge Street
Toronto, Ontario
(416) 486-0512

LE CHOCOLATIER
413-A Spadina Road
Toronto, Ontario
(416) 487-5722

HOUSE OF FUDGE
10-2295 Stevenage Drive
Ottawa, Ontario
(416) 523-6065

HOUSE OF FUDGE LTD.
242½ Bank Street
Ottawa, Ontario
(416) 234-3330

LE FEUVRE'S CANDIES LTD.
683 Mt. Pleasant at Soudan
Toronto, Ontario
(416) 483-5512

SMILES'N CHUCKLES LTD.
1500 Birchmount Street
Toronto, Ontario
(416) 751-3631

TREATS
82 Bloor West
Toronto, Ontario
(416) 922-5181

MANUFACTURERS & DISTRIBUTORS

A & A AMJARV SWEETS LTD.
602 Yonge Street
Toronto, Ontario
(416) 922-5346

BOWES CO. LTD.
75 Vickers Street
Toronto, Ontario
(416) 239-3571

CADBURY SCHWEPPES POWELL INC.
Cadbury Division
170 Attwell Drive
Rexdale, Ontario
(416) 675-2922

CAILLER
c/o Walter E. Jacques Co.

CLAYTON'S HOMEMADE CANDIES
1283 Gerrard East
Toronto, Ontario
(416) 461-7820

DIVA CHOCOLATIER
110 Bloor Street West
Toronto, Ontario
(416) 968-3683

EXCELSIOR BRANDS LTD.
40 St. Regis Circle
Downs View, Ontario
(416) 630-4006

GERHARD'S
Bellamy Road
Toronto, Ontario
(416) 266-9116

GODIVA CHOCOLATIER
The Eaton Centre
Toronto, Ontario
(416) 593-5789

LAURA SECORD CANDY SHOPS
Billings Bridge Plaza
Ottawa, Ontario
(416) 737-5695

LAURA SECORD LTD.
P.O. Box 1812
Station D
Scarborough, Ontario
(416) 751-0500

ROWNTREE MACKINTOSH CANADA LTD.
72 Sterling Road
Toronto, Ontario
(416) 535-2181

TEUSCHER
20-A Hazelton
Toronto, Ontario
(416) 961-1303

TOBLER-SUCHARD
c/o David Ashley & Company

THE ULTIMATE TRUFFLE
4 Colborne Street
Thornhill, Ontario
(416) 881-6959

WILLIAM NEILSON LTD.
277 Gladstone Avenue
Toronto, Ontario
(416) 534-6592

WORLD'S FINEST CHOCOLATE CANADA LTD.
Campbellford, Ontario
(705) 653-3590

Quebec

RETAILERS

ANDREÉ CHOCOLATS
5328 Park Street
Montreal, Quebec
(514) 279-5923

LA BONBONNIERE ENRG.
Place Bonaventure
Montreal, Quebec
(514) 866-0090

BONBONS GUAY LTEE.
Complexe Desjardins
Montreal, Quebec
(514) 843-6321

BONBONS LAURENTIDE INC.
480 Avenue du Parc
Ville des Laurentides
Ste. Anne Des Plaines, Quebec
(514) 478-0666

BONBONS PAUL INC.
12530 Rivoli
Montreal, Quebec
(514) 332-2739

CHEZ TUTTI INC.
5184 de la Reine Marie
Montreal, Quebec
(514) 488-8896

CHOCOLAT JEAN & CHARLES INC.
3187 St. Jacques
Montreal, Quebec
(514) 935-9671

CHOCOLAT PERFECTION INC.
95 Brodeur
Longueuil, Quebec
(514) 468-9282

LA CHOCOLATERIE MIMI-PRIX
5831 Verdun
Montreal, Quebec
(514) 769-6607

LES CHOCOLATS EXQUIS
Place Bonaventure
Montreal, Quebec
(514) 866-9239

LES CHOCOLATS SPLENDID LTEE.
5392 Park
Montreal, Quebec
(514) 279-6473

MANUFACTURERS & DISTRIBUTORS

AKUTAGAWA CONFECTIONERY CO., LTD.
c/o Morris International

ANTHON BERG CHOCOLATES
c/o Morris International

LE BONBON EXPERT LTEE.
3615 Industrial Boulevard
Montreal, Quebec
(514) 323-2121

CHANTILLY CHOCOLATERIE ENRG.
6855 Clanranald
Montreal, Quebec
(514) 731-5473

CHOCOLATERIE CORNÉ TOISON D'OR
La Tulipe Noire
Alcan Building
1188 Sherbrooke Street West
Montreal, Quebec

CHOCOLATERIE GALLER
c/o Godon Closset Ltee.
(514) 688-4570

CHOCOLATS MAXIME
1427 Amherst
Montreal, Quebec
(514) 522-9411

LES CHOCOLATS VENEZIA LTEE.
8810 Champ d'Eau
Montreal, Quebec
(514) 327-4106

JOINVILLE CHOCOLAT LTEE.
5490 Chapleau
Montreal, Quebec
(514) 523-0836

LAURA SECORD CANDY SHOPS
Le Centre Commercial Forest
Montreal, Quebec
(514) 327-1976

PERUGINA
8765 Pascal Gagnon
St. Leonard, Quebec
(514) 327-1656

REGAL IMPORTS CANADA INC.
1755 Berlier
Chomedey, Quebec
(514) 687-2730

SAROTTI CHOCOLATES
c/o I.D. Foods

STILWELL'S HOMEMADE CANDY
5123 Wellington
Montreal, Quebec
(514) 766-4481

SUCHARD
c/o Simon Imports Ltd.

Saskatchewan

A & H CAFE & CONFECTIONERY
Main Street
Holdfast, Saskatchewan
(306) 488-2107

CARENE'S CANDIES
38-134 Primrose Drive
Saskatoon, Saskatchewan
(306) 934-6909

DIAL CONFECTIONERY
Main Street
Lipten, Saskatchewan
(306) 336-2232

UNITED STATES
Alaska

ENCORE CONFISERIE
Captain Cook Hotel
5th and K Streets
Anchorage, AK
(907) 276-5735

NORDSTROM'S
603 D Street
Anchorage, AK
(907) 279-7622

California

RETAILERS

BEVERLY'S BONBONNERIE
330 East 2nd Street
Los Angeles, CA
(213) 687-0528

BIT OF SWEETLAND
8560 West 3rd Street
Los Angeles, CA
(213) 275-5895

CAFE AU CHOCOLAT
2189 Union Street
San Francisco, CA
(415) 922-0716

THE CANDY JAR
210 Grant Avenue
San Francisco, CA
(415) 391-5508

CHAMPAGNE CHOCOLATES & FLOWERS INC.
1832 Buchanan Street
San Francisco, CA
(415) 922-7311

CHOCOLATE-CHOCOLAT DU MONDE
421 North Rodeo Drive
Beverly Hills, CA
(213) 276-7975

CHOCOLATE FANTASY
838 Grant Avenue
San Francisco, CA
(415) 956-5265

CHOCOLATE HEAVEN
Pier 39
San Francisco, CA
(415) 421-1789

CITY SWEETS
1200A Polk Street
San Francisco, CA
(415) 771-6406

CONFETTI LE CHOCOLATIER
4 Embarcadero Center
San Francisco, CA
(415) 362-1706

KAYLAH CHOCOLATIER
598 Downtown Plaza Mall
Sacramento, CA
(916) 448-7178

MOTHER ESTIE
8248 Louise Avenue
Northridge, CA
(213) 705-8311

MANUFACTURERS & DISTRIBUTORS

AKUTAGAWA CONFECTIONERY COMPANY, LTD.
c/o Toha Trading, Inc.

ANDRÉ'S CONFÍSERIE SUISSE
898 Santa Cruz Avenue
Menlo Park, CA
(415) 325-4776

APHRODITE CONFECTIONS OF LOVE
7411 Count Circle
Huntington Beach, CA
(714) 848-6747

CHOCOLATES FROM CHOCOLATES
218 Church Street
San Francisco, CA
(415) 431-3640

COCOLAT
3324 Steiner Street
San Francisco, CA
(415) 567-9957

EDELWEISS CHOCOLATES
444 North Canon Drive
Los Angeles, CA
(213) 275-0341

GHIRARDELLI CHOCOLATE CO.
1111-139th Avenue
San Leandro, CA
(415) 483-6970

GODIVA CHOCOLATIER, INC.
Crocker Center Galleria
San Francisco, CA
(415) 982-6798

GUITTARD CHOCOLATE CO.
10 Guittard Road
Burlingame, CA
(415) 697-4427

JERBEAU HANDMADE CHOCOLATES
2350 South Robertson Boulevard
Los Angeles, CA
(213) 204-0703

KRON CHOCOLATIER, INC.
9529 Santa Monica Boulevard
Beverly Hills, CA
(213) 278-4061

LILED'S CANDY KITCHEN
1318 Tennessee Street
Vallejo, CA
(707) 643-7425

LISA LERNER CHOCOLATES
2984 San Pablo Avenue
Berkeley, CA
(415) 843-5445

MOREAU & PIERRE KOENIG CHOCOLATES
2660 Bridgeway
Sausalito, CA
(415) 332-4621

NEUCHATEL CHOCOLATES
The Century Plaza Hotel
2025 Avenue of the Stars
Century City, CA
(213) 556-1052

NEUHAUS (U.S.A.) INC.
3333 Bristol Street
Costa Mesa, CA
(714) 979-1667

OSOGUD CANDIES
P.O. Box 186
Baldwin Park, CA
(213) 962-7121

PERNIGOTTI
c/o Fabio Imports

THE SAN FRANCISCO CHOCOLATE COMPANY
564 Castro Street
San Francisco, CA
(415) 552-8181

TEUSCHER
9548 Brighton Way
Beverly Hills, CA
(213) 276-2776

VALENTINE'S COSMOPOLITAN CONFECTIONS
1112 4th Street
San Rafael, CA
(415) 456-3262

VAN HOUTEN
c/o Artisto International, Inc.

Colorado

RETAILERS

THE CANDY BAR
Crossroads Shopping Center
Boulder, CO
(303) 440-4857

LE CHOCOLAT
Larimer Square
1430 Larimer Street
Denver, CO
(303) 623-2949

THE CONFECTIONARY
Heritage Square
Golden, CO
(303) 278-1711

FAVORITE THINGS
633 Broadway
Boulder, CO
(303) 499-8497

MANUFACTURERS & DISTRIBUTORS

ANDRÉ'S CONFISERIE SUISSE
370 South Garfield Street
Denver, CO
(303) 322-8871

BERNICE CANDY COMPANY
5335 East Colfax Avenue
Denver, CO
(303) 388-3375

District of Columbia

RETAILERS

LA BONBONNIERE
1919 Pennsylvania Avenue, NW
Washington, DC
(202) 466-6677

CANDY PARLOUR & CONTINENTAL CAFE
1361 Connecticut Avenue, NW
Washington, DC
(202) 861-0638

CHEZ CHOCOLAT
1101 Connecticut Avenue, NW
Washington, DC
(202) 833-3250

CHOCOLATE CHOCOLATE
3222 M Street, NW
Washington, DC
(202) 338-3356

THE CONFECTIONERY
1625 K Street, NW
Washington, DC
(202) 638-0059

ESSENTIALLY CHOCOLATE
1669 Columbia Road, NW
Washington, DC
(202) 387-6994

EXECUTIVE SWEET
1990 K Street, NW
Washington, D.C.
(202) 331-7941

THORNTON'S ENGLISH CHOCOLATE SHOP
National Place Shopping Center
1331 Pennsylvania Avenue
Space 302
Washington, DC
(202) 737-0424

MANUFACTURERS & DISTRIBUTORS

GODIVA CHOCOLATIER, INC.
3222 M Street, NW
Washington, DC
(202) 342-2232

KRON CHOCOLATIER
5300 Wisconsin Avenue, NW
Washington, DC
(202) 966-4946

Connecticut

MUNSON'S CANDY KITCHEN
P.O. Box 224
Bolton, CT
(203) 649-4332

LINDT CHOCOLATES
77 West Putnam Avenue
P.O. Box 2314
Greenwich, CT
(203) 629-2380

Florida

CLOETTA
c/o J.B. & Associates

THAT'S MY FAVORITE
P.O. Box 39387
Fort Lauderdale, FL
(305) 491-4675

Georgia

RETAILERS

THE CANDY GALLERY
1073 Burton Drive, NE
Atlanta, GA
(404) 458-7558

FOUR SEASONS CHOCOLATES
107 Main Street
Atlanta, GA
(404) 921-8321

HAPPY HERMAN'S
Perimeter Mall
Atlanta, GA
(404) 394-0353

JUST CHOCOLATE LIMITED
3393 Peachtree Road, NE
Atlanta, GA
(404) 233-1717

LE CHOCOLAT ELEGANT
3393 Peachtree Road, NE
Atlanta, GA
(404) 233-1336

MANUFACTURERS & DISTRIBUTORS

GODIVA CHOCOLATIER, INC.
3500 Peachtree Road, NE
Atlanta, GA
(404) 233-4461

Illinois

RETAILERS

LEOPOLD'S FINE CHOCOLATES & CONFECTIONS LTD.
6430 North Central Avenue
Chicago, IL
(312) 763-5003

TINGALING CHOCOLATE SHOP
42 West Division Street
Chicago, IL
(312) 752-0825

MANUFACTURERS & DISTRIBUTORS

CUNIS CANDIES
1030 East 162nd Street
South Holland, IL
(312) 596-2440

GODIVA CHOCOLATIER, INC.
Water Tower Place
845 North Michigan Avenue
Chicago, IL
(312) 280-1133

KRON CHOCOLATIER
835 North Michigan Avenue
Chicago, IL
(312) 943-8444

LE CHOCOLATIER
One Magnificent Mile
North Michigan Avenue
Chicago, IL
(312) 943-5582

LONG GROVE CONFECTIONERY CO.
140 East Walton
Chicago, IL
(312) 642-1684

MADAME CHOCOLATE
1940-C Lehigh Avenue
Glenview, IL
(312) 729-3330

THORNTON'S ENGLISH CHOCOLATE SHOP
Oakbrook Mall
Store 96
Oakbrook, IL
(312) 850-7471

J.W. THORNTON LIMITED
845 North Michigan Avenue
Water Tower Place, 5th floor
Chicago, IL
(312) 266-3415

120 West Golf Road
Woodfield Mall, Suite 200
Schaumburg, IL
(312) 843-0340

Louisiana

RETAILERS

CHOCOLATES ELEGANTE
3301 Veterans Memorial Boulevard
Metairie, LA
(504) 835-3311

DANTE STREET DELICATESSEN
736 Dante Street
New Orleans, LA
(504) 861-3634

THE SUGAR & SPICE COMPANY
500½ St. Peter Street
New Orleans, LA
(504) 522-5516

TENDER LOVIN' CHOCOLATES INC.
3009 18th Street
Metairie, LA
(504) 837-7131

MANUFACTURERS & DISTRIBUTORS

EVANS CREOLE CANDY FACTORY CO.
848 Decatur Street
New Orleans, LA
(504) 522-7111

KRON CHOCOLATIER
Uptown Square
New Orleans, LA
(504) 866-1855

NEUCHATEL CHOCOLATES
109 Vermilion Street
Lafayette, LA
(318) 234-7872

Massachusetts

RETAILERS

A EPICURE INC.
59 Causeway
Boston, MA
(617) 742-3734

BAILEY'S OF BOSTON INC.
Faneuil Hall Marketplace
Boston, MA
(617) 523-5025

BITTERSWEET
1647 Beacon Street
Brookline, MA
(617) 232-5117

THE CANDY CONNECTION LTD.
1154 Boylston Street
Brookline, MA
(617) 739-5877

CONFETTI
79 Union Street
Newton, MA
(617) 964-6883

SERENADE CHOCOLATES
324 Harvard Street
Brookline, MA
(617) 566-2225

SWEET PRESENTATIONS
1376 Beacon Street
Brookline, MA
(617) 566-3330

SWEET STUFF
353-C Faneuil Hall Marketplace
Boston, MA
(617) 227-7560

SWEET TEMPTATIONS
Copley Place Mall
100 Huntington Ave.
Boston, MA
(617) 424-0605

THORNTON'S ENGLISH CHOCOLATE SHOP
88 Copley Place
100 Huntington Avenue
Boston, MA
(617) 437-7884

MANUFACTURERS & DISTRIBUTORS

CATHERINE'S CHOCOLATES
Stockbridge Road
R.D. No. 2
Box 32
Great Barrington, MA
(413) 528-2510

Main Street
Stockbridge, MA
(413) 298-4009

Rte. 7
Lenox, MA
(413) 673-1406

CONNELLEY'S CANDIES
333 Union Street
Lynn, MA
(617) 598-2810
(617) 598-8869 (store)

HARBOR SWEETS
P.O. Box 150
Marblehead, MA 01945
(617) 745-7648

MERCKENS CHOCOLATE CO.
P.O. Box 434
Cambridge, MA
(617) 491-2510

NEUCHATEL CHOCOLATES
The Westin Hotel
Copley Place
10 Huntington Avenue
Boston, MA
(617) 424-0684

NICHOLS CANDY, INC.
Rust Island
Gloucester, MA
(627) 283-9850

STOWAWAY SWEETS
154 Atlantic Avenue
Marblehead, MA
(627) 631-0303

Minnesota

RETAILERS

LA BONBONNIERE
7600 Parklawn Avenue
Minneapolis, MN
(612) 831-2101

CHEZ CHOCOLAT
Ridgedale Mall
12561 Wayz Boulevard
Minnetonka, MN
(623) 542-8363

Rosedale Mall
66th & Frances Avenue South
Minneapolis, MN
(612) 636-4555

THE CHOCOLATE PARTY
4946 Cedar Avenue South
Minneapolis, MN
(612) 722-6364

DARVEAUX CONFECTIONNAIRE
201 South East Main Street
Minneapolis, MN
(612) 378-1216

MME LARCELE
200 Third Avenue North
Minneapolis, MN
(612) 343-0289

MANUFACTURERS & DISTRIBUTORS

GODIVA CHOCOLATIER, INC.
1645 South Plymouth Road
Minnetonka, MN
(612) 545-6226

NANOU CHOCOLATES
c/o Larcele Enterprises

REGINA'S FINE CANDIES
248 South Cleveland
St. Paul, MN
(612) 698-8603

Missouri

ANDRÉ'S CONFISERIE SUISSE
5018 Main Street
Kansas City, MO
(816) 561-3440

ANDRÉ'S SWISS CONFISERIE AND TEA ROOM
1026 South Brentwood Boulevard
St. Louis, MO
(314) 727-9928

KARL BISSINGER'S FRENCH CONFECTIONS
4742 McPherson Avenue
St. Louis, MO
(314) 361-0647
(in Missouri, Alaska, and Hawaii)
1-800-325-8881 (elsewhere)

MAVRAKOS CANDIES
4711 Delmar Street
St. Louis, MO
(314) 361-7000

MERB'S CANDIES
4000 South Grand Street
St. Louis, MO
(314) 832-7117

PRICE'S FINE CHOCOLATES
P.O. Box 86
Kansas City, MO
(816) 931-4422

Nevada
ETHEL M CHOCOLATES
P.O. Box 18413
Las Vegas, NV
(702) 877-2777
(800) 634-6584

New Jersey
CIRCUIT CHIPS
Byteware, Inc.
P.O. Box 6725
Lawrenceville, NJ
(609) 882-5769

DROSTE USA LTD.
45 Kulick Road
Fairfield, NJ
(201) 882-0955

GABRIELLE'S FINE CHOCOLATES
5 East Pleasant Avenue
Maywood, NJ
(201) 368-1738

REGINA CHOCOLATES
c/o Cortco International Corporation, Inc.

SAROTTI
c/o Hubbs Importing Corp.

SPRENGEL
c/o C.&J. Willenborg, Inc.

New Mexico
NEUCHATEL
306 Main Street
Clovis, NM
(505) 762-0362

New York

RETAILERS
BALDUCCI'S
424 Sixth Avenue
New York, NY
(212) 673-2600

BREMEN HOUSE
220 East 86th Street
New York, NY
(212) 734-2500

DDL FOODSHOW
444 Columbus Avenue
New York, NY
(212) 787-6644

DEAN & DELUCA
121 Prince Street
New York, NY
(212) 431-1691

ELLEN'S CHOCOLATES
1165 Madison Avenue
New York, NY
(212) 288-1600

FAYE & ALLEN'S FOOD HALLS
1241 Third Avenue
New York, NY
(212) 794-1101

PEPPERMINT PARK
666 Fifth Avenue
New York, NY
(212) 581-5938

PLUMBRIDGE CONFECTIONS & GIFTS
30 East 67th Street
New York, NY
(212) 744-6640

SWEET TEMPTATION
128 West 57th Street
New York, NY
(212) 757-5318

TREAT SHOP INC.
533 Third Avenue
New York, NY
(212) 683-8566

UNIVERSAL CHOCOLATES
2149 Broadway
New York, NY
(212) 874-0630

WINTER'S CHOCOLATIER
826 Lexington Avenue
New York, NY
(212) 308-5655

ZABAR'S
2245 Broadway
New York, NY
(212) 787-2000

MANUFACTURERS AND DISTRIBUTORS

ALETHEA'S
3180 Bailey Avenue
Buffalo, NY
(716) 825-3403

ANTON BERG CHOCOLATES
c/o Morris National

ASTOR CHOCOLATE CORP.
48-25 Metropolitan Avenue
Glendale, NY 11385
(212) 386-7400

CAILLER CHOCOLATES
c/o Jaret International, Inc.

CHOCOLATE PHOTOS
200 West 57th Street
Suite 1106
New York, NY 10019
(212) 977-4340
(800) 262-0024

CHOCOLATERIE CORNÉ TOISON D'OR
725 Fifth Avenue
New York, NY
(212) 308-4060

CHOCOLATES BY M
61 West 62nd Street
New York, NY
(212) 301-0777

CHOCOLATERIE GALLER
c/o Marique Enterprises Ltd.

CONFISERIE SUISSE
Huttmacher Chocolates
40-32 162nd Street
Flushing, NY
(212) 445-9011

ELITE CHOCOLATES
c/o Israeli Assorted Confections (I.A.C.)
350 Fifth Avenue
Room 5315
New York, NY
(212) 563-4895

GENSACO MARKETING, INC.
153 East 43rd Street
New York, NY
(212) 697-3708

GODIVA CHOCOLATIER, INC.
701 Fifth Avenue
New York, NY
(212) 593-2845

HOFBAUER VIENNA, LTD.
P.O. Box 1850
Murray Hill Station
New York, NY
(212) 980-4964

KRON CHOCOLATIER
506 Madison Avenue
New York, NY
(212) 486-0265

LA VIOLETTE CHOCOLATIER
6114 Riverdale Avenue
Bronx, NY 10471
(212) 548-8251

LE CHOCOLATIER
Hotel Pierre
New York, NY
(212) 371-2252

LE CHOCOLATIER
19 South Pearl Street
Albany, NY
(518) 434-1709

LE CHOCOLATIER MANON
872 Madison Avenue
New York, NY
(212) 288-8088

LEONIDAS/D'ORSAY
c/o Pink Imports Inc.

LI-LAC CHOCOLATES, INC.
120 Christopher Street
New York, NY
(212) 242-7374

MICHEL GUÉRARD CHOCOLAT
261 Madison Avenue
New York, NY
(212) 697-3708

MONDEL HOMEMADE CHOCOLATES
2913 Broadway
New York, NY
(212) 864-2111

MOTTA CHOCOLATES
c/o Ferrara Foods & Confections

MRS. LONDON'S BAKESHOP
33 Phila Street
Saratoga Springs, NY
(518) 584-6633

NEUCHATEL CHOCOLATES
1369 Avenue of the Americas
New York, NY
(212) 489-9320

NEUHAUS (U.S.A.) INC.
97-45 Queens Boulevard
Suite 503
Rego Park, NY
(212) 897-6000

NORDCHOKLAD
c/o Atalanta Corporation

PARON CHOCOLATIERS INC.
1149 Third Avenue
New York, NY
(212) 734-7660

PERUGINA CHOCOLATES
637 Lexington Avenue
New York, NY
(212) 688-2490

REBER KUGELN
c/o George C. Brown's Biscuit & Confections
Inc.

RONSVALLE'S
205 Cannon Street
Syracuse, NY
(315) 478-0089

STORK'S PASTRY SHOP
12-42 150th Street
Whitestone, NY 11357
(212) 767-9220

TEUSCHER CHOCOLATES
620 Fifth Avenue
New York, NY
(212) 246-4416

Ohio

GALERIE AU CHOCOLAT
Ross International Confections, Inc.
One Lytle Place
621 Mehring Way
Suite 2209
Cincinnati, OH
(800) 543-7679

HARRY LONDON CANDIES, INC.
1281 South Main Street
North Canton, OH
(216) 494-2757
(800) 321-0444 (outside Ohio)

JOSIP KRAS
c/o Tina, Son & Co.

Pennsylvania

CONFISERIE SUISSE
225 South 17th Street
Philadelphia, PA
(215) 735-5999

GODIVA CHOCOLATIER, INC.
650 East Neversink Road
Reading, PA
(215) 779-3792

THE MAILLARD CORPORATION
1300 Stefko Boulevard
P.O. Box 1158
Bethlehem, PA
(215) 867-7568

NESTLÉ
The Chocolate Collection from Nestlé
Dept. 350
Ronks, PA
(800) 345-8500

REGINA LEE'S CANDIES
1509 Foulkrod Street
Philadelphia, PA
(215) 537-5735

WILBUR CHOCOLATE COMPANY, INC.
Lititz, PA
(717) 626-1131

Rhode Island

NEUCHATEL
176 Bellevue Avenue
Newport, RI
(401) 846-0786

South Carolina

NEUHAUS (U.S.A.) INC.
Harborside II
Hilton Head Island, SC
(803) 785-3545

Texas

ANDRE'S CONFISERIE SUISSE
2515 River Oaks Boulevard
Houston, TX
(713) 524-3863

NEUCHATEL CHOCOLATES
Loew's Anatole Hotel
2201 Stemmons Freeway
Dallas, TX
(214) 651-9508

NEUHAUS (U.S.A.) INC.
Galleria/Dallas Parkway
Dallas, TX
(214) 392-0281

THE SWEET SHOP
2104 West 7th Street
Fort Worth, TX
(817) 332-7941

TEUSCHER
5085 Westheimer
2675 Galleria 2
Houston, TX
(713) 961-4032

Utah
CUMMINGS STUDIO CANDIES
679 East Ninth South
Salt Lake City, UT
(801) 328-4858

Washington
THE DILETTANTE INC.
416 Broadway East
Seattle, WA
(206) 329-6463

DUCZ'S VIENNESE PASTRY & CANDY SHOP
425 South West 152nd
Seattle, WA
(206) 243-4138

ELIZABETH SHAW
c/o Christopher Reeves Brookes & Co.

MILTON YORK FINE CANDIES
P.O. Box 416
Long Beach, WA
(206) 642-2352

PIKE PLACE MARKET CHOCOLATE FACTORY
1918 Pike Place
Seattle, WA
(206) 623-2121

SWEET SWISS
South 5013 Dorset Road
Spokane, WA
(509) 838-1334

Wisconsin
TOBLER-SUCHARD
1400 East Wisconsin Street
Delavan, WI
(414) 728-3403

EUROPE

BENDICKS OF MAYFAIR
Moorside Road
Winnall
Hampshire, SO23 7SA
England

CHOCOLATERIE BRUYERRE
6200 Gosselies
Belgium

CADBURY LIMITED
Bournville
Birmingham B30 2LU
England
021-458-2000

CHARBONNEL ET WALKER
One The Royal Arcade
28 Old Bond Street
London, W1X 4BT
England
01-629-4396
01-629-5149

A. DRIESSEN CHOCOLADEFABRIK
4825 A.P.
Breda, Holland

FORTNUM & MASON PLC
Piccadilly
London W1A 1ER
England

FOUQUET
22 rue Francois ler
75008 Paris
723-30-36

J & A FERGUSON LIMITED
26 Clydesmill Drive
Carmyle
Glasgow
Scotland
041-641-2136

MAYNARDS OF LONDON
Vale Road
London, N41PH
England
01-800-4221

JOSEPH TERRY & SONS LIMITED
The Chocolate Works
Bishopthorpe Road
York, YO1 1YE
England

J.W. THORNTON LIMITED
Derwent Street
Belper
Derbyshire, DE5 1WP
England
077-382-4181

Molds

MAID OF SCANDINAVIA
3244 Raleigh Avenue
Minneapolis, MN
(800) 328-6722

MADAME CHOCOLATE
1940-C Lehigh Avenue
Glenview, IL
(312) 729-3330

ALLMETAL
CHOCOLATE MOLD CO., INC.
1264 Viele Avenue
Bronx, NY
(212) 991-0292

Importers

ARISTO INTERNATIONAL, INC.
P.O. Box 428
San Dimas, CA
(714) 599-6428

DAVID ASHLEY & CO.
3767 Nashua Drive
Mississauga, Ontario
(416) 678-7900

ATALANTA CORP.
17 Varick Street
New York, NY
(212) 431-9000

CHRISTOPHER REEVES BROOKES & CO.
P.O. Box 11107
724 Erickson Avenue
Bainbridge, WA
(206) 842-8518

GEORGE C. BROWN'S BISCUIT &
CONFECTIONS, INC.
1621 Eastchester Road
Bronx, NY
(212) 824-5610

CORTCO INTERNATIONAL CORP., INC.
318 Jefferson Street
Newark, NJ
(201) 589-2236

EXCELSIOR BRANDS LTD.
40 St. Regis Circle
Downs View, Ontario
(416) 630-4006

FABIO IMPORTS
P.O. Box 3593
Redondo Beach, CA
(213) 316-1592

FERRARA FOODS & CONFECTIONS, INC.
195 Grand Street
New York, NY
(212) 226-6150

GODON CLOSSET LTD.
Dumouchel 1665
Laval, Quebec
(514) 667-6809
(514) 668-2546

HUBBS IMPORTING CORP.
436 Old Hook Road
Emerson, NJ
(201) 261-0033

I.D. FOODS
1800 Autoroute
Laval, Quebec

ISRAELI ASSORTED CONFECTIONS
350 Fifth Avenue
Room 5315
New York, NY
(212) 563-4895

WALTER E. JACQUES CO.
P.O. Box CP 261
Hamilton, Ontario
(416) 522-7791

JARET INTERNATIONAL, INC.
2670 Stillwell Avenue
Brooklyn, NY
(212) 946-1800

J.B. & ASSOCIATES
4000 North Orange Blossom Trail
Orlando, FL
(305) 291-1591

LARCELE ENTERPRISES
P.O. Box 4304
Garden Court Station
Minneapolis, MN
(612) 343-0289

MORRIS INTERNATIONAL
1261 rue Shearer
Montreal, Quebec
(514) 931-7525

MORRIS NATIONAL
8 Bond Street
Great Neck, NY
(516) 773-3778

PINK IMPORTS INC.
56 Warren Street
New York, NY
(212) 406-9270

SIMON IMPORTS LTD.
2705 Bates
Montreal, Quebec
(514) 737-1107

TOHA TRADING INC.
3906 Collis Avenue
Los Angeles, CA
(213) 221-4210

C. & J. WILLENBORG INC.
P.O. Box 231
Ramsey, NJ
(800) 526-5342

Glossary

Ballotin: French word meaning "box." Fine Belgian, Swiss, and French chocolates are often packaged in these attractive soft-sided paper cartons.

Bitter Chocolate: Hardened chocolate liquor, a form of chocolate without sugar. Used primarily for baking and candymaking.

Bittersweet Chocolate: (Also known as "semisweet"). Chocolate containing a minimum of sugar. Used for baking, candymaking, and eating.

Bulk Chocolate: See "couverture."

Caramel: Mixture of sugar, water, and fat (such as butter). Used as filling in candy.

Chocolate Liquor: Dark, thick liquid paste that is the end product of grinding cocoa beans.

Coating Chocolate: See "couverture."

Cocoa: Crushed, ground, and sifted cocoa beans from which the cocoa butter has been removed.

Cocoa Butter: Vegetable fat that is a by-product of the processing of cocoa beans. Used in chocolate manufacture and in the cosmetics industry.

Conching: Process by which chocolate is refined over a period of time by heavy rollers that smooth the chocolate mass (which sits in a large trough).

Couverture: Also called "coating" or "bulk" chocolate. Has extra cocoa butter, which makes it shinier, softer, and smoother. Used by confectioners and chefs, but also desirable for eating. Sold in large blocks.

Crème Fraîche: Raw whipping cream that is allowed to mature naturally. When whipped, sweetened, and flavored, is used as a filling for chocolates, particularly in Belgium and France.

Croquant: French term for caramelized sugar plus crushed nuts. Gives chocolates a crunchy quality.

Fondant: Basis of "cream" fillings. Consists of whipped sugar, glucose, and flavorings or extracts. Basic color is white, but natural and artificial coloring is often used to tint it.

Ganache: Filling consisting of cream, butter, and chocolate with sugar. Serves as a basis for truffles.

Gianduja: Filling consisting of finely ground hazelnuts or almonds, sugar, milk, and chocolate.

Marzipan: Melted sugar plus finely ground almonds, combined to form a paste.

Milk Chocolate: Chocolate liquor plus sugar, cocoa butter, vanilla (or vanillin, an artificial flavoring), and at least fourteen percent milk solids.

Nougat: Also called "torrone." Whipped egg whites combined with boiled sugar, honey, almonds, nuts, and candied fruit.

Praline: 1. Pronounced "prah-lee-neh." European term of German origin, meaning fine chocolates of any description. 2. Pronounced "pray-lean." Finely ground hazelnut or almond filling.

Semisweet Chocolate: See "bittersweet chocolate."

Torrone: See "nougat."

Truffles. A blend of chocolate, butter, sugar, and cream, filled with ganache, liqueur, or fruit flavorings, and rolled in cocoa powder or powdered sugar. Their free-form shape resembles that of the black fungus truffle, for which it is named.

White Chocolate: A blend of cocoa butter, sugar, and vanilla or vanillin. Many do not consider this "real" chocolate because it does not contain chocolate liquor. A boon to those allergic to chocolate.

Bibliography

Ambrosia Chocolate Co. *Food of the Gods*. Milwaukee, WI, 1983. This pamphlet, first published in 1945, tells the story of cocoa and chocolate in an entertaining, if not highly sophisticated, manner. Its old-fashioned illustrations are charming.

Boynton, Sandra. *Chocolate, the Consuming Passion*. New York: Workman, 1982. A whimsical view of chocolate facts and trivia featuring marvelously witty cartoon illustrations.

Chocolate Manufacturers Association of the U.S.A. *The Story of Chocolate*. McLean, VA, 1978. Another look at chocolate, from cocoa beans to the finished delicacy, with some interesting and heartening information on chocolate and health.

Cook, L. Russell. *Chocolate Production and Use*. New York: Magazines For Industry, 1972. A comprehensive view of chocolate from a detailed technological standpoint.

Crown Publishers. *The New Larousse Gastronomique*. New York: Crown, 1977. Fascinating historical information about the popularization of cocoa and chocolate throughout Europe and the Americas.

Heatter, Maida. *Maida Heatter's Book of Great Chocolate Desserts*. New York: Knopf, 1980. The famed dessert chef's collection of her favorite chocolate recipes, plus tips on how best to work with the wonderful stuff. Not for dieters!

Kolpas, Norman. *The Chocolate Lovers' Companion*. Twickenham, England: Felix Gluck Press, 1977. A compendium of amusing anecdotes and facts about chocolate, plus a discussion of chocolate's contribution to literature.

Leaver, Alex. *Making Chocolates*. Walnut Creek, CA: Weathervane Books, 1975. Practical information about how to practice the art of chocolate confectionery–making in one's own home.

Marcus, Adrienne. *The Chocolate Bible*. New York: Putnam, 1978. A confirmed chocoholic's nominations for chocolate greatness, with descriptions of her visits to master chocolate makers' factories.

Minifie, Bernard W. *Chocolate, Cocoa and Confectionery: Science and Technology*, 2d ed. Westport, CT: AVI, 1980. Everything you always wanted to know about the science of chocolate making. For the serious chocolate lover who wants to be better informed about how chocolate becomes chocolate as we know it.

Rinzler, Carol Ann. *The Book of Chocolate*. New York: St. Martin's Press, 1977. Facts and fancy about chocolate, plus suggestions about how to improve one's chocolate tasting ability.

Union of Swiss Chocolate Manufacturers. *Chocologie*. Bern, Switzerland, n.d. A highly informative, good-humored discussion of cocoa and chocolate making in general, and the Swiss chocolate industry in particular. Full-color photographs (especially of the mouthwatering chocolate sculpture which opens the chapter on "Swiss Chocolate Pioneers") add to the fun and tempt the palate. Some recipes are also included.

Index